COLLEGE COMPOSITION AT MIAMI

LEIGH GRUWELL, EDITOR
RENEA FREY, ASSISTANT EDITOR

EDITORIAL ASSISTANTS
KATHLEEN COFFEY
DUSTIN EDWARDS
GRETCHEN DIETZ
MORGAN LECKIE
KEELY MOHON
SARAH MORRIS
JONATHAN RYLANDER
JOHN SILVESTRO
ALYSSA STRAIGHT

DEPARTMENT OF ENGLISH

MIAMI UNIVERSITY
HAMILTON • MIDDLETOWN • OXFORD

Including College Composition at Miami Digital
Companion Site at: http://ccm.miamiu.haydenmcneil.com

2013–2014, Volume 66

Hayden-McNeil Sustainability

Hayden-McNeil's standard paper stock uses a minimum of 30% post-consumer waste. We offer higher % options by request, including a 100% recycled stock. Additionally, Hayden-McNeil Custom Digital provides authors with the opportunity to convert print products to a digital format. Hayden-McNeil is part of a larger sustainability initiative through Macmillan Higher Ed. Visit http://sustainability.macmillan.com to learn more.

Hayden-McNeil Publishing
14903 Pilot Drive
Plymouth, MI 48170
www.hmpublishing.com

Palmeri 5815-3 F13 (College Composition at Miami)

Department of English Directory
Department of English Main Office
356 Bachelor Hall
Miami University
Oxford, OH 45056

Director of Composition
Dr. Jason Palmeri
356A Bachelor Hall

If you need further information or if you have questions about College Composition at Miami University, contact the Composition Office at (513) 529-5221.

The *CCM* staff would like to thank the students who offered their work to this project. We would also like to thank the English Composition instructors who encouraged their students to submit essays for consideration.

Table of Contents

Welcome Letter from your CCM Editorial Board

Dear Miami Writer,

The book you're holding right now is like no other textbook you've ever seen before. Okay, that may be a bit of an exaggeration - but it *is* unique. Why? Because it was composed by Miami student writers like you! As teachers and as writers ourselves, we respect your composing processes and value your voice. This, the 66th volume of *College Composition at Miami*, aka the *CCM* as we fondly call it, reflects just how important we feel your voice truly is in building this foundational text for our composition classes here at Miami University.

The reflections, public arguments, critical essays, and multimedia projects published in this book were authored by students enrolled in Miami's English 109, 111, and 112 courses. Each year, our editorial board comes together to select works that demonstrate sophisticated and compelling approaches to the types of assignments you may be asked to tackle in your composition classes. The projects published are the result of multiple drafts, critiques, and revisions. We did not choose these particular pieces because they earned "A's" or because they are "perfect"; rather, we feel that they each have a great deal to offer you in terms of learning about writing and composing here at Miami University and in your civic and professional futures.

Although we have included our own notes and questions, as well as reflection letters from the published student writers themselves to help guide your thinking about each essay and project; really, this book is about *your* writing and what aspects of the texts included can inform, influence, and improve the work you produce. As you read, always consider what you can learn from the student voices you find here. Instead of viewing the compositions as "models" to imitate, ask yourself "How do these authors approach building introductions, crafting thesis statements, supporting ideas and arguments, and critically engaging with the culture and community around them? And how might I do the same in my own college writing?" Reading the work of your peers, we hope, will inspire you to take risks in your writing, to thoughtfully respond to feedback from your instructor and your classmates, and to experiment through multiple drafts toward your best intellectual work.

One of the things we know can come from this process and your use of the *CCM* is an ability to consider the world around you and how it shapes your identity, views, and values more carefully. You'll be told repeatedly, no doubt, as you progress through your composition courses that learning how to "think critically" is a key goal of Miami University writing classes. This is true, and we say, there is no better way to develop this skill than by writing. F. Scott Fitzgerald—you know him: the guy who wrote *The Great Gatsby*. Remember reading that in high school? Or going to see the movie last summer? He once claimed that "You don't *write* because you want to *say something*, you *write* because you *have something to say*." We hope that this book - combined with the readings, assignments, and class discussions of English 109, 111, and 112 may not only help you find your something to say but will also help you to say it more effectively.

This *CCM* has more in it than just thought-provoking and useful student projects. It is also a guidebook on how to successfully navigate your composition classroom. Your instructor is possibly the most valuable resource for any questions you may have about writing or the course. But we think this book can be very beneficial, too. We've included tools for understanding the composing process valued at Miami University as well as additional resources that can help you improve your writing. You'll find tips on how to use Miami University's library systems, how *not* to use someone else's intellectual property, and where to find campus-wide writing centers, among other priceless gems of information.

Just so you know...this *CCM* extends beyond the pages of this book. We have even more examples of writing that you can make use of on our online version. You can check out the *CCM* archives and additional   2013-2014   picks   at http://ccm.miamiu.haydenmcneil.com.This book also exists as a pretty awesome souvenir of your experience here at Miami. Take a look at the cover. These tiled instagram images were taken by intrepid faculty members, hoping to reflect your experiences as student writers at Miami. For our next edition, you'll create the cover. Because let's face it, you're cooler than any faculty member ever could be. This cover is just one example of how the images and texts you see in this book represent campus perspectives and capture your college community.

To help your friendly editorial board build next year's "souvenir" and to take advantage of the opportunity this publication offers you to voice your own perspectives and experiences, we encourage you to contribute (seriously, do it) tweets of instagram images, insights, memorable classroom moments, commentary on late night revisions - whatever you have to say about your world and your writing - to the cover title hashtag, #*thisisMUcomp*. We also hope you will submit one or several of the essays and/or projects you create in your English 109, 111, or 112 classes to the Composition awards committee this academic year! You can use this simple online form: https://www.units.muohio.edu/engcomp/. It only takes a minute to fill out and submit, so why not? You could be featured in this book next year. Also, there are prizes.

We look forward to reading your contributions and we are eager to see how your writing challenges or innovates in ways that we don't yet find in this current book. After all, you - yes, *you* reading this right now - make *College Composition at Miami* what it is. Your writing, your process, your voice - your tweets and photos and academic prose - *this* is MU Composition.

Here's to an epic year of writing and thinking together!

Your 2013-2014
Editorial Team

How to Use the CCM

You may be asking yourself what the point is of reading the student essays published in the *CCM*, or wondering how reading work that other students have written for different classes can help you. Why does Miami publish student essays and then make other students read them? How does this work?

These are fair questions, and when reading through these essays there are some approaches you can take that may make these readings more helpful and actually assist you in making your own writing more effective. When reading through the essays in the *CCM*, try to note your own reactions to the writing. Are you bored? Interested? Irritated? Delighted? What do you like or dislike about the pieces that you read? And more specifically, *why* might you be reacting the way that you do? What is the author doing or saying that evokes these feelings? Conversely, what is it about *you* that interacts with the writing in these ways?

Second, how effective do you find the writing to be? Are you convinced by the argument? What evidence, appeals, or supporting points did you find the most persuasive? Why? When you step back and consider these questions, you may then examine *how* the writer has accomplished this. What rhetorical moves "work" within the paper to enhance the overall effect of the writing? By analyzing the work of other students – especially work that is considered particularly effective – you may be able to step back and figure out what about that writing makes it successful.

When you examine these essays, consider not only their content or topics, but also aspects of the writing such as style, voice, arrangement, persuasive appeals, evidence, transitions, organization, etc. If an essay is particularly appealing to you, ask yourself what the author is *doing* in that piece that you find so compelling. By engaging in this process of analysis, you develop a skill called *meta-cognitive awareness*, which means thinking about a thinking (or writing) process so that you gain an understanding of not only *what* is being said, but *how* it is being said and *why* that is or is not effective for a given audience in a particular situation. Likewise, you can apply this skill to your own writing, asking many of the same questions, and thus figuring out how *you* write and what you may be able to do to make that even more effective.

You may also want to review the goals or outcomes for each Inquiry before you read an essay so that you can apply your skills of analysis to thinking about why and how a particular essay meets these goals, or even asking how it could have done so more effectively. What does the author do? What strategies or approaches are employed that you may be able to utilize in a different context? You can also read the Reflective Letters included before each essay – what does the author say about the writing process to produce that work? What might you take away from it that you can apply to your own process? Also, at the end of each essay is a short note from the editors of the *CCM* discussing aspects of the essay that we found interesting, compelling, or particularly effective. In addition, we may ask questions for your consideration while reading the essay that may also lead to you figuring out how the *CCM* can work to help you produce effective writing in your own classes and assignments.

The goal of the *CCM* is not to promote the idea of "copying" or "imitating" a particular essay, but rather to encourage meta-cognitive awareness of various rhetorical moves that can make writing more effective. When reading these essays, keep these ideas in mind and think of other questions or ways of interrogating these pieces. In this way, we hope that the *CCM* will work for you, to help you compose, analyze, and understand your own writing processes.

The Writing Process

We at the *CCM* and in the English Department view writing as a process. That is, writing is not a one-off activity--you write the essay, and you're done. If you want your writing to improve, it requires planning and practice and exploration. It requires drafts and revisions. It requires time. However tempting it may be to wait and write a paper the night/morning before it is due, your writing will reflect the fact that you were under stress. As former and current students ourselves, we can tell you from experience that the products of stress are rarely our best work. Arguments develop holes; organization is non-existent; and, in general, brains are fried. The writing process allows you the opportunity to save your brain and develop well-thought out and coherent essays.

While the ideal writing process varies from person to person, your writing instructor will introduce you to and ask you to practice several different steps: prewriting, research, drafting, peer response, conferencing, revising and editing, and publishing. It is important to note that the writing process is not linear. You do not smoothly progress from prewriting to publishing. It is messy. You may prewrite, draft, prewrite some more, conduct peer response, revise, conference, prewrite, revise, and, finally, publish. You may be doing some of these steps at the same time. Your writing process may change with each new essay. Don't get frustrated. The more you write and the more you practice, the more comfortable you will be with the fact that there is no one right way to write, but there is the way that works for you.

Prewriting:
Prewriting is a useful way to generate topics and ideas that you can use in your writing. Once you receive the assignment from your instructor, you can use one of the multiple prewriting methods to get you started and past the horror that is the "empty white page." Here are a few examples:

- listing: If you are stumped, create a list. It's a good idea to have a question in mind that the list is answering. For example, "What topics could I use to answer the assignment question?", "What do I already know about my chosen topic?", "What are some questions that I want my essay to answer?".

- freewriting: Set a time limit, usually 5-10 minutes. During this time write non-stop about the assignment or your chosen topic. Your hand should be moving constantly, and you should not worry about mistakes. Don't look back. If you can't think of anything, you write "I can't think of anything. I can't think of anything. This is kind of annoying. Why does Instructor M wear her hair like that? I can't think of anything" until you can think of something and move on. You can build on freewrites by pulling out useful information from one to help start another.

- clustering/webbing: You might have done this in high school. Write the topic in the center of your paper. Draw lines out from the topic and write down related ideas and details. Branch out from those and add more related ideas and details. Eventually, you should have what looks like a web. Clustering/Webbing can be very helpful with organization since you can physically see the connections that occur between your ideas.

- questioning: Use the reporter's questions to interrogate your topic: Who? What? Where? When? Why? How? You can make the questions more sophisticated to fit your topic, but once you have answers to your initial questions, begin again by interrogating the new information you have collected. This can be extremely useful if you think you have covered every angle and run out of ideas.

- outlining: Many prewriting methods create a jumble of excellent but disconnected ideas. Outlining allows you to put those ideas into a coherent order. First, you decide what your major topics are and the most logical order in which to arrange them. Then, you decide under which topic each of the subtopics you generated belongs, again deciding the most logical order in which to arrange them. You can also use this method to help you decide where you may need more support from outside sources. A detailed outline can help make writing your first draft faster and easier.

- multimodal prewriting methods: Not all of your prewriting needs to be done with pen and paper. A *Prezi* or *PowerPoint*

Presentation can help you boil down your ideas into the main points and can make it easy for you to visually rearrange elements to see where they fit best. If you work better with images than with words, <u>image clustering</u> may be more helpful than the clustering method mentioned earlier. In this method, you collect images that represent the major themes and ideas of your project, placing related images closer to each other. If you like to talk through your ideas instead of writing them down, consider <u>audio recording</u> so that you will not lose the ideas you gain.

Also, it is important to remember that in 109/111 and 112 you will be asked to create multimodal projects. As you may have guessed, multimodal describes a process or project that utilizes multiple modes of communication, such as text, sound, and images. Multimodal projects include videos, radio broadcasts, websites, posters, and storybooks to name a few. If you choose to create a video, <u>storyboarding</u> can allow you to map out each scene in your project. Draw a series of squares representing each scene. In the squares, you can draw the main layout of the scene. It doesn't have to be anything beautiful. We've found that stick figures work quite well. Under each square, you can write the dialogue, action, music, color scheme, etc. Between squares, you can write notes about transitions or text screens. The more detailed you are in the storyboard, the less you have to worry about as you put together the final project. <u>Visual outlining</u> works well if you are creating a static project like a poster or advertisement. It can also be used to outline the content on a webpage. While this method is similar to storyboarding, it asks for more detail concerning what images will be included and where; the type of information that will be included in text, what that text will look like, and if it will be hyperlinked; the colors that will be used and the emotional response the colors will excite in the reader.

A writing journal or blog can help you keep track of all of your prewriting. Don't forget to go back and use what you have already done.

Research:
Miami offers a wide range of research materials both online and through the various libraries on campus. (See "University Libraries" in the Resources section for more information.) Research can be used as a prewriting method. For example, you could create a list of what others have already written about your topic and find new areas to explore. If you discover two authors who disagree with each other about your chosen topic or question, you could create a pretend conversation between them where you anticipate how each would respond to the ideas of the other. Research can also be used after prewriting to help support your ideas or offer counter-arguments in your work. It is a good idea to use multiple sources to support each of your main points instead of relying on only one source for each point. This shows that you have delved deeply into your topic and have considered the views of all relevant authorities.

Your instructor will likely set guidelines for the types of materials you will be allowed to use in your essays. Pay careful attention to these guidelines because failure to do so could lead to the use of unreliable sources that weaken your essay and result in a lower grade. Usually instructors ask that you use academic journals, news sources, and books from the library, but be sure to check your writing prompt or ask your instructor concerning the appropriateness of your sources. Another important thing to remember is to use the sources you find ethically. (See the next section, Working with Sources/Avoiding Plagiarism, for information on the ethical use of sources.) You will learn how to analyze the relevance and authority of sources and how to cite sources correctly throughout 109/111 and 112.

Drafting:
Keep in mind that there is a reason we usually call these "rough" drafts. They are an initial attempt at putting your thoughts into essay format and testing how the ideas you generated through prewriting will fit together. While your draft should be thoughtful, it does not have to be polished. Usually you will be offered the chance to create and improve multiple drafts of your essay based on feedback from peer response and conferences with your instructor. Do not get too attached to your draft, as you will probably receive advice that requires you to make substantial changes to the organization, argument,

or sources. While this can be painful, it does wonders for strengthening your essays and improving your ability to foresee potential issues on your own in the future.

When you begin a draft of your essay, you should have access to all of the prewriting and research materials you have collected. Find a location where you think you will be productive, a place that is comfortable and allows you to focus. Some people work well in their dorm rooms because they can work through the noise and the comings and goings of their roommates. Other people need the quiet offered by the library.

When you begin to write, don't feel like you have to start with the introduction. Introductions tend to be the most difficult part of the essay to write, so starting with a working thesis and then going back to write the introduction will save you the stress of having to find that perfect opening line. Also, remember that you don't have to do everything in one sitting. Some people work better if they write for an hour or two and then take a break. It can give you a chance to consider what you have already written. By starting early and approaching writing as a process, you avoid the stress of having to get it right the first time, or exhausting yourself staying up all night finishing a draft that will probably not be your best work anyway. By giving yourself time for a process-based writing experience, you may find that writing is less stressful, more enjoyable, and leads to more successful outcomes.

Peer Response:
Getting feedback from others can be extremely helpful during the drafting process. Although there are many different ways of conducting peer response, most instructors will ask you and your classmates to read through each other's writing and give advice for how to improve the work. While you may give and receive some comments on grammar, spelling, and sentence structure, the main purpose of peer response is to test the larger issues, such as the appropriateness of the tone for the intended audience, the organization of the ideas, the strength of the argument, and the relevance of the sources.

Many students feel unqualified to help their classmates with their writing. However, remember that you offer a fresh look at your classmates' writing and may be able to see their topic from a different background and perspective. Constructive responses to your peers' work should be respectful and go beyond statements of "This is good" or "This is bad". Also, avoid comments that sound like demands--" Fix your organization." Not only does this comment sound somewhat hostile, it does not give the writer a clear idea of how to "fix" the issue. Instead, offer workable suggestions that explain why you think a change should be made and how it could be done. For example, "If you move paragraph four to after paragraph one, this could help with the transition between your major ideas." Where demands create resistance, suggestions create conversation and consideration that could lead to improvement. Finally, don't forget to tell the writer what you think they do well. Encouragement can be just as useful as suggestions and can show the writer what they should continue to do in the future.

Conferencing:
Conferencing is another way to receive feedback on your writing. All instructors will read through your drafts and offer comments and suggestions in the margins or at the end of the essay, but, on major papers, they may also ask you to meet with them to discuss your work. This gives you a chance to respond to and receive clarification on your instructor's comments. It's a good idea to prepare two or three questions before you go to the conference because time will be limited. Even if conferences are not required, you may find it helpful to set up an appointment with your instructor to go over your draft and to get feedback in this way prior to turning in your paper.

Revising and Editing:
Revising and editing are two different steps. Revising refers to changes that you make to the larger issues mentioned above: tone, organization, argument, sources, etc. These changes may include, but aren't limited to, adding new information, rearranging paragraphs, deleting unnecessary sections, and replacing weak information with stronger information. Editing refers to smaller changes to elements like grammar, sentence structure, and word choice. It is a good idea to begin with revision and save editing until you are preparing the final

draft. That way you will avoid wasting your time fixing sections you may delete or change anyway. Your instructor will lead you through in-class activities and homework assignments to help you approach revision for each major inquiry assignment.

Publishing:
This is the final step in the writing process. Eventually, you will have to stop writing and revising and give your writing to an audience to read or grade. The writing process never really comes to an end; it is merely stopped by deadlines and ends of semesters.

All of the entries included in the *CCM* are the products of a writing process and illustrate the points made above. While they are polished, they are not "complete." As you read the writer's letters for each *CCM* entry, you will notice that many of the authors not only explain the specific process they used to write their essay, they also mention elements that they would still like to change. This is normal and an expected part of the writing process. When you begin to prepare drafts for your college writing assignments, you may refer back to some of the advice and insights offered by students who have contributed to the *CCM*, or what advice you may have to offer other students in the future. In this way, the writing process is carried on, not only within individual assignments, but from student to student, from year to year, through the composition courses here at Miami.

Working with Sources/Avoiding Plagiarism

Writing is a social endeavor. When we write, we essentially are collaborating with other people—their words, ideas, arguments, styles, and so forth. While this is true for all writing, it becomes especially clear with research genres of writing. In essence, research consists of building upon and enhancing the work of others. As such, keeping track of sources is an essential practice for exchanging, expanding, and constructing knowledge. Throughout your college career and beyond, understanding how to ethically and responsibly account for others' work will be an important skill to continue to develop.

Understanding Plagiarism

As a student, you've likely experienced the "plagiarism talk"—the *thou-shall-not-plagiarize* speech often given at the start of classes or at the outset of a major research project. The talk, although somewhat intimidating, is given for good reason. Plagiarism is a serious matter—not just for students but also for public officials, literary authors, scholars, journalists, and many others. Plagiarism can cause damage to a person's reputation and integrity as well the institution in which the person works.

In academic contexts, plagiarism is a major breach of academic integrity that can have serious consequences for those who are charged of it. Severe violations of academic integrity—such as submitting a purchased essay or lifting large chunks of non-cited texts—can result in the failure of the assignment or the course. It's likely you already know this. The consequences for easily identifiable forms of plagiarism are often discussed during the "plagiarism talk" or are stated in course syllabi. But it may not be as clear as to why the consequences are so strong. Deceptive forms of plagiarism, those where writers are intentionally passing off others' work as their own, disrupt the work of collaboration. In this way, plagiarism stalls the research process and, perhaps more importantly, the learning experience gained from collaborating with others' work.

Understanding Patchwriting and the Gray Areas of Plagiarism
While there are easily identifiable types of plagiarism (those that aim
to deceive), we have found that students are often more anxious navigating the not-so-clear types of plagiarism. Have you ever noticed that
when you work with new or complex texts, it becomes difficult to put
particularly challenging information within the context of your own
paper? Writing educator Rebecca Moore Howard has identified a
strategy many use to integrate complicated texts into their own work.
She calls this strategy patchwriting. Essentially, patchwriting is pulling in sentences from a source and replacing a few words with
synonyms and/or slightly changing the grammatical structure in an
effort to rephrase the source language. We find patchwriting is often
used when writers feel unfamiliar or uncomfortable with source material. Although many see patchwriting as part of learning how to
research complex ideas, it is worth knowing some instructors perceive
patchwriting as a type of plagiarism. In other words, patchwriting, in
some instances, can have the same consequences as plagiarism. If you
feel like you're drawing on source material too closely, it's a good idea
to rethink your strategy. If you can't get away from the source language, think about quoting it. Otherwise, take a step back and think
about what the source is saying overall. How can you fit it within the
context of your own paper? Perhaps try rephrasing the information
using several different variations--then choose the one that works best
for you.

Navigating the gray areas of plagiarism can be complicated. To help
you through the process, below we respond to some commonly asked
questions we have encountered from students:

How often do I need to cite? As a general rule, any time you directly use
a source (by direct quotation, summary, or paraphrase), you should
provide attribution. This involves both citing the source in text and
providing bibliographic information in the Works Cited (MLA) or
Reference (APA) page. Also, when using a source throughout your
work, be sure to cite it every time. This may seem redundant at first,
but try to think of citing sources as interacting with them not simply
plugging in names. Also, there are ways to vary how you cite a
source; for instance, think about using different signal phrases (i.e.
Jones states, the author writes, according to Gonzales, etc.). We have

found that sometimes students think placing one parenthetical citation at the end of a paragraph suffices for attributing sources within the whole paragraph. This simply is not true. Be in dialogue with your sources throughout the paragraph.

Can I still be accused of plagiarism even if I provide a citation? The short answer is yes. Avoiding plagiarism involves providing *accurate* in-text and bibliographic citations. Be sure to double-check your sources to make sure you're attributing the correct author for his or her work. Further, be sure to cite the source using the particular style guide you're writing in (i.e. APA, MLA, Chicago, etc.).

How do I determine "common knowledge?" Unfortunately, there are no clear-cut rules for discerning common knowledge. The task of determining whether or not to cite will always be contextual. There are, however, some approaches you can take to help make your decision. Notice some of the moves we're making. We open this section with a fairly specific claim—"writing is a social endeavor." Although this claim can likely be attributed to certain thinkers (the Russian theorist Mikhail Bakhtin, for example), we feel no need to cite specific sources for a couple of reasons. For one, this claim is largely accepted within academic communities. Second, we are not directly building off of or responding to a certain author's work. As such, the claim, we believe, constitutes common knowledge. However, later in this section, we attribute a specific term, patchwriting, to a particular person, Rebecca Moore Howard. We cite Howard largely because she coined patchwriting, a term not known by many. Also, we actively build from Howard, suggesting, like Howard does, that patchwriting is a strategy used by writers unfamiliar with particular texts.

How rigidly should I follow certain style guides (such as MLA or APA)? Style guides are meant to help with the research process. They provide writers a kind of shorthand, allowing them to easily look up works of interest if they want more information. Because finding, building upon, and expanding past works is the central goal of most academic work, a unified system of keeping track of sources is important. Undoubtedly, different teachers and disciplines are going to have varying expectations about following style guides, but we think it's good practice to try to follow them as closely as possible. If you're stuck, many resources, such as the Purdue OWL and for-purchase stylebooks, exist to help you work within style guidelines.

What are other ways to reduce plagiarism? When working with a lot of sources, keeping track of who said what can be overwhelming. To avoid confusion, it's always good practice to keep track of the sources you're using or thinking about using. Think about keeping a detailed research journal or a continually updated annotated bibliography to keep your sources organized.

Complicating Matters with Digital Media

When composing digital media, as with Inquiry 4 for English 109 and 111, thinking about using others' work in a *legal* manner is also paramount. While most legal and writing specialists make important distinctions between plagiarism (an ethical transgression determined by academic and discipline communities) and copyright infringement (a legal violation determined by U.S. federal law), both involve working with other people's work in an irresponsible manner. Key to understanding how to avoid copyright infringement is an awareness of fair use.

The fair use doctrine allows composers to use portions of copyrighted materials without having to ask the copyright holder for permission. This right, as stated in Section 107 of the U.S. Copyright Act of 1976, essentially allows you to legally incorporate others' work (portions of images, videos, songs, etc.) in your own compositions. However, in order to adhere to fair use guidelines, there are some things you need to know. Legal scholars Patricia Aufderheide and Peter Jaszi argue that most court rulings have seen uses as fair when they are "transformative" in nature. In other words, composers who seek to offer something new — to transform — copyrighted works are typically within their fair use rights. Consider, for example, Jonathan McIntosh's remix "Buffy vs. Edward: Twilight Remixed." McIntosh's video remix uses clips from both the television series *Buffy the Vampire Slayer* and the movie *Twilight* to create a new narrative. McIntosh essentially re-writes *Twilight's* main character, Bella, to highlight the patriarchal themes present in Edward and Bella's relationship. McIntosh's remix is likely to be seen as fair because of its transformative nature — not only does it use short clips but it also offers commentary and critique.

To get a more detailed understanding of your rights, the following criteria are often used when determining whether a use is fair:

- The purpose or character of the use. How and for what reasons are you using the copyrighted work? Educational purposes or commercial ones?
- The nature of the copyrighted work. Is the copyrighted work a creative text or a more journalistic, fact-driven text?
- The amount and substantiality of the portion used in relation to the whole of the work. How much of the copyrighted work are you using?
- The effect on the potential market of the copyrighted work. Will your use hurt the sales of the copyrighted work?

Like quoting others' words, employing fair use is a way to offer critique, construct knowledge, and exchange ideas. If claiming fair use, you are more likely to be within your rights if your work is produced for noncommercial purposes. Importantly, fair use is your right. Don't be afraid to use it. In fact, Aufderheide and Jaszi compare fair use to a muscle. "Fair use becomes real only when people actually use it," they write, "like a muscle, it can shrink with disuse" (xi). That said, if you want to use free licensed material—texts where you wouldn't have to contemplate fair use—there are plenty of online resources available, such as Creative Commons, ccMixter, and Archive.org.

Remember digital composers can still plagiarize even if they are within fair use guidelines (e.g. using short portions of works without citing them). And conversely, composers cannot plagiarize and still be tried for copyright infringement (e.g. citing sources accurately yet failing to adhere to fair use guidelines). In short, to be a responsible user of others' work, be sure to 1) cite your sources and 2) use those sources in a manner cognizant with the fair use doctrine.

Tips on Working with Sources
1.   When in doubt, ask your instructor. Plagiarism is determined socially—meaning, instructors, administrators, disciplines, particular codes of ethics, and so forth, have slightly different expectations for

responsible source use. If you're unsure about something, it's always best to double-check with your instructor. We're here to help.

2. Work *with* sources, not *from* them. This is a small distinction, but we think it's an important one. If you find yourself attempting to patch in individual sentences from a book or journal article, you are likely not in dialogue with the source. This usually gets writers into trouble. It's better to have a solid understanding of a source — meaning, you've read and comprehended it — rather than mining unread sources for quotes or particular passages.

3.   Give yourself time. Research — from brainstorming your agenda, gathering your information, reading your sources, and drafting your paper — takes a lot of time and work. In our experiences, the potential to use sources in an ethical and responsible manner is heightened when writers take the necessary time to do research.

4.   Be a thorough note keeper. Contrary to popular belief, annotated bibliographies are not assigned to make your life miserable. When working with sources, it's always a good idea to annotate what you've read to keep track of which source said what. In writing your annotations, be sure to distinguish your language from the source's language.

5.   Familiarize yourself with the genre you're writing in. We have found instances of plagiarism increase when students are unfamiliar with genre expectations. Our best advice here is to read examples, be sure you understand what you're being asked to do, and ask questions if you have doubts. It's also useful to think about ways you can intervene in the genre in a way that makes sense to you. For example, when reading examples of rhetorical analyses, think about ways you can take charge of the assignment while still maintaining the outcomes of a rhetorical analysis.

6.   Understand the differences between copyright infringement and plagiarism. Plagiarism is an ethical violation; copyright infringement is a legal violation. To avoid plagiarism, be sure to cite all the sources you use — including images, sound files, video clips, and so on. To avoid copyright infringement, be sure to use others' work in a trans-

formative way, following the guidelines of fair use. Otherwise, use public domain or licensed materials (from websites such as Creative Commons, CCmixter, and Archive.org).

7. Be aware of plagiarism but don't let anxiety deter you from writing. Remember that writing—especially writing for specialized academic audiences—takes practice. No one is born a researcher or a writer. Understanding how to avoid plagiarism is a practice developed over time.

Penalties
For a discussion of plagiarism penalties, see your course syllabus, talk to your instructor, or visit Miami University's Academic Integrity Web site at http://www.miamioh.edu/integrity/.

Plagiarism Avoidance Web Resources:
"Plagiarism Avoidance," Purdue Owl:
http://owl.english.purdue.edu/owl/resource/930/01/

"What Is So Important About Academic Integrity?" International Society for Academic Integrity:
http://www.youtube.com/watch?v=xSfmWIlEhSg

"Citation Resources and Guidelines," Miami University Libraries:
http://libguides.lib.muohio.edu/citation

Works Cited
Aufderheide, Patricia, and Peter Jaszi. *Reclaiming Fair Use: How to Put Balance Back in Copyright.* Chicago: U of Chicago P, 2011. Print.

Howard, Rebecca Moore. "A Plagiarism *Pentimento.*" *Journal of Teaching Writing* 11.3 (1993): 233-246. Print.

McIntosh, Jonathan. "Buffy vs Edward: Twilight Remixed." Online video clip. *YouTube.* YouTube, 19 June 2009. Web.

Resources

University Writing Opportunities

Writing for the *CCM*

As we mentioned in our Welcome to you, the English Department and the editorial board to recognizes and celebrates your exemplary writing every year. We've created various award categories that are reviewed by a committee of qualified faculty and graduate students. We look forward to reading your contributions and considering your work for Composition Awards and/or publication in the *CCM*. Submitted work should be revised, perhaps incorporating your instructor's comments and suggestions. If you decide to contribute your work, please remember to submit an accompanying Writer's Reflection.

There are two venues for showcasing your outstanding writing: *College Composition at Miami* (*CCM*) –the book you're holding—and the online companion to the *CCM* (visit it at http://ccm.miamiu.haydenmcneil.com/).

In these venues, the Composition Program publishes English Department Award winners as well as other innovative and exemplary examples of student writing that build this primary course text. You may submit any compositions from English 108, 109, 111, or 112 courses.

The Awards Committee considers student writing in the following categories:

- Rhetorical Analysis Award
- Persuasive, Research-Based Argument Award
- Reflective Narrative Award
- Literary Analysis Award
- International Student Writing Award (for an essay from 108 or 109)
- Bedford/St. Martin's Digital/Multimedia Writing Award
- Reflective Portfolio Award

All award winners will receive *at least* $100, distributed either as a check or as a bookstore gift certificate. (Note: Not all of the essays published in the *CCM* have won awards or are eligible for prize money. Only those in designated award categories qualify for this distinction.)

The deadline for awards submissions is March 1st. The deadline for submissions for publication consideration (*CCM* and Web) is the last class day of spring semester. Share the essays, projects, and reflections that you're most proud of and throw your hat in the ring for the *CCM* publication and/or Composition Awards via the online *CCM* or this URL: https://www.units.muohio.edu/engcomp/

In addition, we will also be continuously reviewing the advice, memorable moments, images, and memes, etc. that you share on twitter via the hashtag #thisisMUcomp for possible cover art and in-text publication in next year's *CCM*.

Additional Writing Opportunities
Miami University offers many opportunities for writing outside of your college composition classes. You can submit your writing to other campus publications, such as student and local newspapers: *The Miami Student* (Oxford) and *The Hawk's Eye* (Middletown); literary magazines: *Illuminati* (Middletown) and *Inklings* (Oxford); and student organization newsletters.

Throughout the year, the Joyce and Roger Howe Center for Writing Excellence also sponsors contests and events geared to foster the culture of writing at Miami University. For more information about those awards and how you can submit your work, go to http://writingcenter.lib.muohio.edu/

You can also submit your work to the annual Oxford Writer's Festival through this link. This celebration, put together by students for our Community - including other Miami students, faculty, and Oxford residents - invites local and international authors to present and workshop their writing. To participate, check out their website at: http://oxfordwritingfestival.weebly.com/

Campus Resources

Howe Writing Center

The Howe Writing Center is a valuable resource that you can take advantage of throughout your time at Miami. With five locations (King Library; Windate, in18 Peabody; B.E.S.T Library in Laws Hall; the Gross Center; and, for writing assigned in Farmer School of Business courses, the Howe Writing Initiative in FSB 3064), the Howe is staffed by undergraduate and graduate students from a wide variety of majors. These trained consultants collaborate with you to help you meet your writing goals at any stage of a writing project, from planning to research to revision. Consultants can help you address both higher-order and lower-order concerns, depending on the stage of writing, but most of the time the emphasis is on higher-order, such as audience, organization, and argument. It's important to note that he consultants are not trained as proofreaders/editors. While they're happy to work with specific grammar issues, the center does not provide editing services. To receive personal consultations, you can make an appointment online at http://writingcenter.lib.muohio.edu/

Regional Campus Writing Centers

The Hamilton and Middletown campuses also offer writing center services. Hamilton's Center is located in 108 Rentschler Hall and the Middletown   Center   is   located   in   002   Johnston   Hall (http://www.mid.muohio.edu/studentservices/readingwritinglab.cf m).

Miami University Libraries

Explore the Miami University Libraries – four unique libraries and two archives that offer more than just a lot of books and a quiet place to study. King, Miami's main library, is open 24 hours a day/ 7 days a week during the school year so you can get the information you need any time of day.

Be sure to check out the other library locations on campus: Amos Music Library in the Center for Performing Arts, Wertz Art and Architecture Library in Alumni Hall and our newest library, BEST: Business, Engineering, Science and Technology, located in Laws Hall.

These libraries offer specialized resources and staff for specific majors and classes, but students of any major are welcome to use whichever library they choose.

Library facilities offer computer labs and stations; laptop, iPad and video equipment for checkout; individual and group study rooms; printing; technology help and textbooks for 2-hour checkout. Of course, you can also access millions of books, tens of thousands of sound recordings, magazines and journals and DVDs, including many resources that can be retrieved online or from your cell phone.

Additionally, you can get help researching at any library information desk. Here, librarians can assist you in finding and evaluating sources, navigating library databases, integrating and citing sources, or findings books. Librarians are on hand to help with any research questions you have, for English or any other subject. Research help is available via email, in person, or by text message or instant message. Just send an instant message to miamiulibraries or text a question to the number 513-593-9114. You can also visit: http://www.lib.muohio.edu/askus for all the different ways to get help.

There are excellent library facilities on the regional campuses: Gardner-Harvey Library on the Middletown Campus and Rentschler Library (in Schwarm Hall) in Hamilton. Many of the same resources available on the Oxford campus can be found there as well.

All students, no matter what campus or time of day, can access a wealth of resources through the Libraries' website: http://www.lib.miamioh.edu. Becoming a frequent visitor of the Libraries (in person or online) can greatly enhance your experience at Miami. The libraries' resources and services can benefit your research, writing and academic skills as a first-year student and beyond.

If you would like to contact a librarian about an English assignment or any other project, your best resources are Lindsay Miller, First Year Experience Librarian (mille234@miamioh.edu and 513-529-8035), or Arianne Hartsell-Gundy, Humanities Librarian (hartsea@miamioh.edu and 513-529-8494).

English 104 and 105: Writing Studio
If you think you would like additional help working through your writing assignments for your composition class, or any other courses you may be producing written work, consider signing up for a section of ENG 104 or 105. The Writing Studio course is a small-group, one-hour elective that you may take at any point in your academic career.

In a Writing Studio course the focus of instruction is on your own and others' writing. The studio leader and your classmates will help you to better understand your writing assignments, your writing goals, and guide you through drafting, revision, and editing processes. The Studio asks you to share your final productions and process materials throughout the semester. In this space, you will to learn to ask critical questions about writings from various disciplines, and engage in wider, more nuanced, conversation about academic writing conventions.

If you're interested in registering in this course, please contact the Director of Composition, Jason Palmeri in Bachelor 356A during the first two weeks of the fall or spring semester.

Useful Online Resource for Writers
Purdue OWL:

http://owl.english.purdue.edu/

Offers resources on writing processes, research, grammar and mechanics, and style. Also includes resources for citing sources in MLA, APA, Chicago, etc. Offers a wide variety of tools for ESL writers.

American Rhetoric:

http://americanrhetoric.com/

A comprehensive collection of influential speeches from historical figures, films, and key political activists. Also includes Platonic, Aristotelian and contemporary definitions of rhetoric. A wonderful place to find primary texts for rhetorical analysis.

Handbook of Rhetorical Devices:

http://www.virtualsalt.com/rhetoric.htm

An online database of key rhetorical terms. Includes definitions and examples to help you better understand the language your instructor may introduce in class.

Career Services
Your first year of college is the perfect time to start thinking about your future! As a first-year student you can join the Career Certificate program and work toward a career certificate that will help you move toward finding a career you will love. Make an appointment with a Career Services advisor, who can help you think intentionally about how you can connect your classes and co-curricular activities at Miami University to your future career aspirations.

If you are not sure what you might be interested in pursuing, head over to http://www.units.muohio.edu/careers/where you can take the Focus2 to learn more about possible career paths. At Career Services, you can get support in exploring summer jobs, internships, and volunteer activities that provide you the skills and knowledge you need to be successful.

Composition Program Policies

AP/Transfer Credit and Portfolio Program
For information about AP and Transfer Credit and the Portfolio Program, visit the composition website at http://www.units.muohio.edu/composition/

Force-Adds for Composition Classes
We try very hard to make sure that every incoming student who needs to take a first-year composition course can find a seat in the course. We cannot, however, ensure your right to a particular section or with a particular instructor. If you have any problems or questions related to your enrollment in ENG 104, 105, 108, 109, 111, and 112, please contact the Composition Director, Jason Palmeri (Bachelor Hall 356A). Instructors are not permitted to force-add students, so until you have met with the Director, do not try to force-add into a class or attend a class section assuming that you will be force-added to it later. **No force-adds or requests for section changes will be considered until the first day of classes each Fall and Spring semester.**

A force-add may be approved for you in a composition course if you have a significant reason for needing to take the course this semester or to change your already assigned section. Such reasons might include:

- You have a work or childcare commitment that creates a conflict with your currently assigned section.
- The room to which you are assigned cannot accommodate your particular learning needs.
- You are not yet enrolled in a required composition course but need to take the course this semester.

Class Attendance
Please be sure to pay close attention to your syllabus and your instructor's attendance policy. Attendance policies for composition courses are often very stringent, because acquiring and developing writing abilities requires a different kind of instruction and learning than in other types of courses at the university. Much of the learning in composition classes happens through "engaged learning" in class: via in-

class inquiry activities, in-class writing assignments, and group inter-action that cannot be easily made up or replicated outside of class. Thus, regular attendance and participation are extremely important to your success and learning in a composition class. For more information, see *The Miami Bulletin Student Handbook*, Chapter 9, "Class Attendance," Section 1.9.A, at

http://www.units.muohio.edu/reg/bulletins/GeneralBulletin2012-2013/

Dropping or Withdrawing from a Course

Please note the procedures and policies regarding dropping and withdrawing from a course. Section 1.2.C of the *Student Handbook* (2012-2013 edition) outlines these specific policies. You can view these online at

http://www.units.muohio.edu/reg/bulletins/GeneralBulletin2012-2013/.

If you are considering either option, you should meet with your instructor and advisor.

Evaluating Your Instructor and Your Course

At the end of every semester, you will have the opportunity to evaluate and provide feedback on your instructor and course. If your instructor fails to provide an opportunity for student evaluations, or if you simply wish to share your observations about the course, please contact Jason Palmeri, the Director of Composition in 356A Bachelor Hall.

If you wish to informally or formally make a complaint about an instructor's teaching practices (for not following the Statement of Good Teaching Practices as defined in section 1.7.A.1 of the *Student Handbook)*, you should contact the English Department Chair, *after* first attempting to resolve the issue directly with your instructor.

Commitment to Campus Safety and Diversity

As a department, we expect Composition instructors and students to strive towards creating a climate that not only encourages learning, but also promotes tolerance, acceptance, and a stimulating intellectual environment for every student. This is the socially just and ethical responsibility of everyone. It is also an explicit learning outcome throughout all composition courses.

We support and work to thoughtfully engage, through critical thinking, the Miami Plan and the University Diversity Statement, both of which have been designed to help students think through ways to live in an increasingly complex social climate and to challenge them to look beyond their own experiences and realities. As The Diversity Statement explains:

> Miami University is a multicultural community of diverse racial, ethnic, and class backgrounds, national origins, religious and political beliefs, physical abilities, ages, genders, and sexual orientations. Our educational activities and everyday interactions are enriched by our acceptance of one another; and, as members of the university community, we strive to learn from each other in an atmosphere of positive engagement and mutual respect. Because of the necessity to maintain this atmosphere, bigotry will not go unchallenged within this community.

Our challenge, then, as members of the Miami University community, is to recognize that diversity exists in many different forms and contexts and to honor the differences people see in each other. Engaging with diversity means not assuming that everyone is the same. Accepting differences involves reading and talking about issues that may not be a part of everyone's life.

We hope you will feel comfortable in your courses and work (with us, with other students, and with other on-campus groups) to create more equitable and safer classrooms (and broader campus spaces). We also hope that you will call our attention to any marginalizing or oppressive situations you or your classmates may face.

Guidelines for Using Non-Sexist Language

Language not only reflects the world around us, but also shapes people's thoughts and attitudes. The way in which people write or speak affects their audience. Words are symbolic acts, so they can harm people every bit as much as physical acts. Our language still contains conventions that in more subtle ways can be just as hurtful as obviously offensive words. Therefore, vocabularies have shifted significantly over the past several decades. Words that unnecessarily label people on the basis of race, religion, class, gender, ethnic origin, disability, or sexual orientation are inappropriate because they're needlessly exclusive.

For instance, if we use the pronouns *he*, *his*, or *him* to represent both men and women, if we use *man* to represent all human beings, or if we label people as *mailman* or *chairman* regardless of their gender, we are using gender-exclusive language. By not being aware that even seemingly insignificant parts of our language (like the use of pronouns) can have a powerful impact on our readers and listeners, we can potentially trivialize or alienate at least half our audience.

Thus, composition instructors ask students to use gender-neutral language in papers written for composition classes. In this policy, the English Department is following the guidelines used in all Miami University publications, as well as in professional journals in academic fields. Using gender-neutral language helps create and maintain a democratic culture.

Professional organizations such as the National Council of Teachers of English and the Modern Language Association have required the use of non-sexist language in their publications for more than a decade. The examples that follow are some ways you can avoid accidentally transmitting gender-biased messages along with the messages you mean to send. Such careful attention directed toward all members of your reading audience makes you a more thoughtful and powerful writer.

Avoid the pronoun problem by using plurals in sentences.
Example: Give each student his paper as soon as *he* asks for it.

Alternative: Give students their papers as soon as *they* ask for them.

Eliminate words that cause unnecessary sex/gender references.
Example: A nurse must take care of *her* patients.
Alternative: A nurse must take care of *the* patient.

Use inclusive nouns.
Example: fresh*man*, *man*kind, chair*man*
Alternative: first-year student, human beings, chairperson

Use alternatives to phrases that marginalize or stereotype women.
Example: lady lawyer, woman doctor, career girl, poetess
Alternative: lawyer, doctor, professional, poet

Sexual Harassment Sexual Assault/Violence Resources

We are very aware of the possibilities of receiving unwanted sexual advances or even abuse, and take these instances very seriously. The editorial board implores you to make known any instances of unwanted sexual advances, sexual harassment, or sexual abuse—either in the classroom or out.

In instances of sexual harassment, you are encouraged to contact the Office of Equity and Equal Opportunity: http://www.units.muohio.edu/oeeo/

If you have experienced any form of sexual assault and/or violence, please contact the Butler County Rape Crisis Program by calling their 24-hour helpline at (513) 523-4146. You may also choose to contact Miami University Police by calling (513) 529-2222 or Oxford Police at 9-1-1. Also be aware of Miami's Sexual Assault Prevention and Response Program: http://www.units.muohio.edu/sexualassault/

GLBTQ Services

The mission of GLBTQ Services is to make the Miami University community an open, safe, and inclusive environment for people of all sexualities and gender identities. They provide programming, support, and resources intended to raise awareness regarding gay, lesbian, bisexual, transgender, and questioning (GLBTQ) issues. For more information, including the opportunity to become as "Safe Zone" member (as a student or teacher) and to view a list of faculty allies, visit the GLBTQ Services website: http://www.units.muohio.edu/saf/glbt/

Disability Services

The Office of Disability Resources (ODR) "provides reasonable accommodations and resources to ensure equal access to education, employment, and University life. Furthermore, ODR is passionate about advancing and sustaining an environment of equal access, diversity & inclusiveness for all members of the University community." Please find more information on the ODR website: http://www.units.muohio.edu/oeeo/odr

Award Essays

ENG 108/109 Award

China's Home Appliance Subsidy Program Should Be Halted
Xiqian Zhu

In recent years, the quantity of Chinese exports has declined as a result of reduced global demand in the context of the global financial crisis. Thus, the Chinese government has focused on its consumer spending in the domestic market instead. To be specific, the Chinese government intends to assist home appliance suppliers in surviving during the global financial crisis and make the Chinese economy develop more rapidly. The home appliance subsidy program offers subsidies for television sets, washing machines, refrigerators, and mobile phones. In addition, the government sets a certain price ceiling with the rebate for consumers in rural areas, and it was officially launched on February 1, 2009 throughout China in order to spur consumer spending in the domestic market. A number of problems resulted from the program; therefore the issue over whether the program should be halted has arisen. This paper will argue that the program should be halted.

The program creates a negative impact on a number of small brands, while name brands benefit from the program. The official currency of China is the renminbi (RMB). The government sets a RMB 2000 (US$315) price ceiling for large-screen television sets, and this price ceiling is beneficial to most large-size flat-screen television set manufacturers, except for small producers. Normally, Jiangsu Baixue and Changling focus on their own niche market, since they have already built their corporate image and reliable reputations in rural distribution; however, the emergence of large-size flat-screen television set producers is a significant threat to small brands. Take Jiangsu Baixue as an illustration. Its sales heavily rely on rural areas. Gu Yixin, the manager of Jiangsu Baixue, indicates that ninety percent of their sales are made in rural areas (Hille). The company is faced with the threat of low revenue so that leading brands gain the opportunity to penetrate the market in rural areas, which has been controlled by indigenous niche players. According to vice director of the China Home Electrical Appliance Association, Jiang Feng, the company that captures the market in the rural area will win the market in the future

(Li). Before the price ceiling was set, rural customers were fond of products of Jiangsu Baixue. As Jiangsu Baixue desperately tried to compete, it has been unable to compete in the face of cheap products from big brands after the program was launched. Consequently, the rural population is naturally attracted to home appliances from leading brands. In other words, small brands lose market share, since a remarkable decrease in the price of products of leading brands makes those brands more attractive to the rural population.

What is also worth noticing is that plenty of leading brands suffer from a price ceiling. The sales manager of Changling complains that smaller and unqualified firms take advantage of the program by claiming that they are eligible to implement this decision making authorized by the Ministry of Finance (Hille). These smaller firms offer lower prices in the market, so the price of other retailers provides is incomparable. For instance, small retailers provided much lower prices that involved thirteen percent rebates. At the same time, rural consumers may be exposed to low-quality home appliances thanks to the high possibility of purchasing unqualified products from these smaller retailers. Other than that, essentially, rural consumers are less immune to information delivered by profiteers compared to urban dwellers, owing to their inherent nature of simplicity and undeveloped living circumstances. The worst thing is that the defective goods are full of potential risks, which in turn may make consumers either need to pay an extra fee for repair or are exposed to electrical short circuits. Although rural consumers may lack the chance to experience the home appliances of name brands, if the program ceases, they would not be hurt. Nevertheless, if the program continues to run, a larger portion of the rural population would suffer from the program in the future.

Furthermore, service provided after sales is another issue. The number of service shops in rural areas is not as prevalent as in urban areas. The supply of accessories is always scarce, or the skill of the staff is low. As the article states, complaint cases involving television sets increased by eleven percent in Shandong, Henan, and Sichuan provinces (Feng). It means that it is not convenient for rural consumers to receive quick, convenient, and effective service. Consumers complain that their homes are far away from the places where their home appliances can be repaired (Li). Unlike rural residents, those who live in urban areas enjoy the most efficient and high-quality service. Restocking is never a problem. In rural areas, a large number of illegal service shops have appeared as a consequence. Rural consumers, who have problems with their home appliances, ask these smaller repair service shops for help, but the quality of repaired service cannot be guaranteed. As a matter of fact, the price of home appliances still accounts for a substantial portion of farmers' incomes; for example, a farmer, Shi Yunguo, considers a TV which costs RMB 1000 (US$157.50) a luxury good (Li), even without extra repair costs. In contemporary Chinese society, most have to deposit money for tuition fees and medical care, especially for medical care, because the health care system in China is deficient. Repair costs can become a burden to farmers.

Admittedly, it is difficult to deny the fact that the home appliance subsidy program acts as a contributing factor that shrinks the gap between urban dwellers and rural residents step by step. Citizens' standard of living is supposed to correspond to China's rapid economic development. A large number of rural residents are able to use modern home appliances and are more likely to benefit from them. A small but persuasive example can be given. Microwaves seemed to be inapproachable before the program was established, whereas rural residents could afford one with the rebate. By analogy, this program is designed for the current economic situation in China. According to *The Washington Quarterly*, China's economy suffers from the rising value of its currency, rising market-based salaries, and inflation in recent years as well as demand under the global sales slump (Overholt). Hence, concentrating on the domestic market is crucial for the Chinese economy to maintain a developing rate, especially in the rural market. The effect that the program creates is impressive. As the *China Chemical Reporter* states, China's sales revenue has been increasing annually. The sales revenue of home appliances in rural areas in 2010 is 1.9 times higher than that in 2009. The effect is expected to be far-reaching in the next several years.

These aspects are generally accepted. Nevertheless, the routine of rural dwellers is not the same as that of urban residents. Rural residents make a living by doing farm work. Normally, they wake up at four or five o'clock in the morning, do farm work until dusk, and then have dinner; that is routine life in the countryside. After that, most are too tired to watch TV. Therefore, TV seems like wastage for farmers. By analogy, air conditioners are considered useless home appliances in rural areas due to exorbitant prices. In farmer Shi's village, only a few residents possess air-conditioners and refrigerators (Li). Most rural residents regard these two home appliances as luxury goods, and prefer to spend money on other useful items instead. Moreover, the utility fee is a burden for many in rural areas. In other words, they can afford home appliances, but they cannot necessarily afford the utility fee. A small but convincing example gives details of the argument: washing machines may facilitate rural life if the utility fee is not taken into account. Therefore, most prefer to wash clothes by hand.

It is clear that the disadvantages of the home appliance subsidy program greatly outweigh the advantages of the program, when biases are cast away. Thus, it is wise to support the end of the home appliance subsidy program. The laudable intentions of the government notwithstanding, the government is too eager to be successful. Alternatively, the government should take other actions to tackle the problem, such as increasing the price ceiling so that it is likely to protect home appliance firms and rural residents from unhealthy competition and potential risks. A price ceiling that is slightly higher than RMB 2000 is worth considering, perhaps RMB 2500 (US$393.75). It will not largely exceed annual rural incomes, and it protects most small and big brands at the same time. In addition, the government should focus on unauthorized repair stores to prevent rural residents from illegal and incompetent service. Purchasing high-qualified second-hand home appliances is beneficial to rural populations as well. It is especially suitable to buying expensive home appliances, such as refrigerators and air conditioners. If these recommendations are followed, rural residents will begin to enjoy more of the benefits derived from modernization.

Works Cited

"China's Domestic Demand Grows Rapidly In November." *China Chemical Reporter*. 22.1 (2011): 6-7. Print.

Feng, Qiuyu. "Compliant For Home Appliance Program Due to Insufficient Repair Centers." *Guangzhou Daily*. 3 Sept. 2009. Web. 3 Mar. 2012

Hille, Kathrin. "Manufacturers Pin Hopes on Rural Families." *Financial Times*. The Financial Times Ltd. 3 Feb. 2009. Web. 14 Feb. 2012.

Li, Yahong. "Home Appliance a Tough Sell in the Countryside." *China Today*. 33.1 (2010): 21-34. Print.

Overholt, Williams H. "China in the Global Financial Crisis: Rising Influence, Rising Challenges." *Washington Quarterly*. 33.1 (2010): 21-34. Print.

Editorial Team's Note

Xiuian Zhu's essay offers a very clear and convincing argument for halting the home appliance subsidy program in China. By using a variety of well-integrated sources, Zhu provides sound reasoning for halting this program, while still presenting multiple sides and counter-arguments, as well as enough background and history so that a reader who is unfamiliar can understand the issue. This essay is focused and specific, using a solid, concrete issue as its basis, and then providing an in-depth, nuanced position and clear call for action. What issues are of interest in your locality or hometown? How might arguments such as these intervene into the public realm to help form policy? By beginning an inquiry into local politics or policies, you may find that your views are able to help form and inform opinions and actions within your communities.

Rhetorical Analysis Award

The Queen's Speech
Matthew Armelli

Writer's Reflection

After writing my second paper for this class I have grown as a writer especially when analyzing a text based on the rhetoric used. The most important thing that I have learned from writing Inquiry 2 is that when I write an analysis of any type I need to leave my emotions and personal opinions out. The point of writing this paper is analyze how the use of speech is or isn't effective not whether I personally thought that the speaker did a good or bad job. Through writing and composing this essay, I have definitely seen the importance of rhetoric and its power to either help someone push their point or to tear down another opponent. Rhetoric is used in our everyday lives and I never realized that I use it every day until I realized that such simple things that I say like when I try to convince my friends to go see a movie or eat at one dining hall rather than another all relies on rhetoric. It is truly amazing how much we use rhetoric and do not even realize that we are. After looking at my revisions and comments about my paper, there are a couple very important changes I made. The most important yet seemingly obvious one is relating everything back to my thesis. I have a great explicit thesis and cannot forget to relate every example back to it so that I can build a strong argument. By revising my topic sentences to always reflect the thesis has helped me reach this goal. Another important topic was my citing of sources. I will use the OWL to help me with correct citing for speeches. Overall, this paper has showed me how to objectively analyze a rhetorical situation and effectively detect the major parts of rhetoric.

◆ ◆ ◆

When the Queen of England gives a speech, the entire world watches to see what she has to say and after years of conflict and hate between Ireland and Great Britain the sight of Queen Elizabeth II in

Dublin was no doubt a powerful one. Her Majesty Queen Elizabeth II spoke to an audience of both British and Irish dignitaries during a state dinner at the historic Dublin Castle. As head of the British Crown and Queen of fifty-four countries, her speech was a huge step in the rebuilding of relations between the two nations. Her Majesty, having reigned for sixty years has experienced the Irish-British conflict first hand with the murder of her uncle by the Irish Republican Army, giving her a direct link to the violence. Queen Elizabeth's visit and speech has been seen by the ever critical media as a forced, insincere attempt at improving relations while the general public see the speech as a giant leap forward in the relations between Ireland and Great Britain. The Queen's ethos, having reigned for sixty years and served in the Auxiliary Territorial Services during World War II proves a strong credential for her. In her speech, she offers her deepest regrets to those who lost loved ones during the conflict but never ceases to push the point of the shared cultural and economic links that both nations need to embrace in order for progress to succeed. Although Her Majesty is not officially a politically powerful figure, her ethos and pathos, especially, delivered a resounding message of hope, unity and progress to those seated inside Dublin Castle on that May evening.

When the Queen opens her speech in Irish Gaelic by saying, "A huachtarain agus a chaired (President and Friends)" she immediately and effectively uses pathos to connect with the audience. The fact that the Queen begins her speech in Irish Gaelic rather than her native tongue immediately shows the extra research and practice she had to have done in order to pronounce the statement correctly. The audience, especially the Irish Prime Minister Mary McAleese, respond with "Wow" and a round of applause signaling their approval of the Queen's attempt. The Queen immediately builds a bridge between herself and the audience due to the pathos used in her opening statements and leaves the way open to continue her message of progress.

The audience is then again given a strong dose of pathos when the Queen addresses the "world-famous hospitality of Ireland." Through this statement the Queen directly says that the Irish people, in spite of all the conflict between the two nations, are at heart a good people. Coming from the Queen of England, whose Uncle was killed by the IRA, truly signifies a lot. The Queen is able to see through the violence and understand the whole picture rather than associating everyone with the violence of the IRA. In her next statement, the Queen possibly makes her strongest case for the progressive relationship between Ireland and Great Britain. She discusses the "shared values", "economic, business, and cultural links" that make the two nations much more than neighbors but rather "firm friends and equal partners." Referring to the Irish as "friends" and "equal partners" the Queen is appealing to the audiences' pathos by calling them equals. This puts them on the same level and allows them to feel that they are all of the same importance in this effort. From past speeches that the Queen has given it is very clear that she rarely says things she does not whole-heartedly believe as shown in her tribute speech to Diana, Princess of Whales.

When Princess Diana died in 1997, the Queen's speech was not given until a week later because she wanted to be there to comfort her grandsons in the grieving process. When Queen Elizabeth II did give the speech "*Diana, Princess of Whales Tribute*", she began by saying that she is speaking to her subjects from her heart as "your Queen and as a grandmother." This strong connection to anyone who has lost someone close to them helps the Queen show the importance of family to her and by taking care of her grandsons before going public further shows her devotion to family first. By saying that she is a Grandmother helps remind the audience that she is a human being with a mother and children and grandchildren just like them and she can feel pain and grief just as deeply as everyone else. Because the Queen took the time to grieve and console her grandsons before talking to the people of Great Britain she allowed herself to speak with a clear mind and give a truly genuine message to the grieving thousands. This is also the case in Ireland.

The Queen is quoted saying in reference to Ireland, "I have to be seen to be believed" (Hardman), which shows her commitment to the resolution of the conflict and that she would rather go to Dublin and speak in person rather than issue a statement apologizing for the losses of those during the violence. The Queen allowed herself to look at the conflict as a whole, like in the Diana tribute speech, and presented both the good and bad but focused mainly on the results of the events. In the Diana tribute speech the Queen hopes that the world will see, "The British nation united in grief and respect" and again uses the concept of unity in Dublin when she says, "These ties of family, friendship and affection are our [Britain and Ireland's] most precious resource." Both speeches repeat the idea of coming together and sharing their grief and memories together in order to move forward. Emphasizing the good that came of both tragic events and the better future that is to come. Unifying the audience with these references to "family", through pathos, reminds the audience of their own family and enforces the concept of the British Isle family that they all are a part of and the need to take care of it just as hard as their own families. For if they do not grave consequences are bound to occur.

Calling the relationship between the two nations as not always being "benign" or "straightforward" brings the thought of cancer into mind and resonates with the audience. Using the thought of cancer helps the two nations see the long- term effects of their turmoil and realize the "heartache, turbulence, and loss" that they have all suffered. All of these harsh and emotional appeals to pathos help to break down the pride that each nation has for itself allowing the Queen to begin to rebuild the relationship from the ashes. She creates an image of unity between the nations appealing to their pathos by saying, "No-one who looked to the future over the past centuries could have imagined the strength of the bonds that are now in place." By giving the audience a new unified pride that will be shared for generations to come definitively builds the hope and optimism for the future-an effective use of pathos.

Although the Queen, having reigned for sixty years and having helped bring England out of the carnage of World War II, has outstanding ethos, she cannot ignore Irish President Mary McAleese if she hopes to fully complete her mission. Her Majesty praises President McAleese for her part in bringing the nations together using such examples as the joint opening of the Messines Peace Park in 1998 to "shed new light on the sacrifice of those" in World War II. This helps the Queen show her admirations for Irish President McAlesse and respect for those all who served in World War II. In a way, she is giving President McAleese the spotlight, which appeals to the Irish audiences' pathos specifically because they are seeing one of their own take initiative in this effort, which in turn inspires them to take action as well. The Queen is using pathos to show the audience that each of them has an integral part in the creation of this new future between the two nations; it is not just her responsibility.

Northern Ireland, a very sore subject between the Irish and British, could have been a very damaging subject for the Queen if not addressed in the right manner, but the Queen's use of pathos magnificently guides the audience together. She describes how thirteen years ago a majority of people in Ireland "voted in the favor of the agreement signed on Good Friday 1988." Connecting this momentous occasion to Good Friday, the day on which Christ was crucified, helps the Queen show first, the respect of Ireland's majority religion (herself belonging to the Church of England) and second, showing the rebirth associated with the decision to create Northern Ireland. Her Majesty calls Northern Ireland an "exciting and inspirational place" which in turn reflects the decision of Ireland to create the nation, a magnificent use of pathos by applauding Ireland's decision. The "inspirational place" is also in reference to the new atmosphere that Britain and Ireland hope to create between themselves, appealing to the audiences' desire for a better relationship between the two nations leading the Queen to a powerful point.

By appealing to the Irish and British pathos when she says, "It [Ireland and Great Britain's peace progress] gives hope to other peacemakers across the world that through sustained effort, peace can and will prevail", the Queen is making Ireland and Britain an example for all peoples around the world who strive for peace. This appeals to the audience as it makes them examples of success to the world and by suggesting this, the Queen is urging the future Irish and British to prevail in this united effort, continuing to the goal of becoming "equals." In the last few minutes of the speech the Queen uses repeatedly the word "shared" as in, "our individual responses will be all the stronger for working together and sharing the load", along with the reference to the solemn history of both nations being "at the heart of our shared narrative" and in reference to the peoples of both countries, "these families [British and Irish] share the two islands." In using the word "share" over and over, the Queen is emphasizing the unity of the nations and illustrating, to the audience, that through years of conflict both nations still have a common background and this can help both nations come to terms with what happened and move forward. Using the word "share", the Queen is effectively using pathos to appeal to the hearts of the audience. With both peoples sharing these "two islands" and having a "shared narrative" the Queen is emphasizing how both nations have a responsibility to take care of the relationship between them since both Ireland and Britain have been so closely intertwined throughout history.

As the world watched the Queen deliver her monumental speech on 8 May 2011, no one could have expected the importance of the Queen's message. Such a respectable and adored figure around the world put national pride aside and embraced the shared and common history of the two nations. Although the media believed her speech was politically motivated and insincere, the courage that she has had during her reign and the countless people she has personally affected prove her sincerity. As Her Majesty says in reference to her everyday letters of well-wishers and birthday cards from the public, "Those letters are written to me and therefore I must read them myself", when she could easily have her staff read and reply to them. She takes her position very seriously and wants to have made a difference when she is done. From the time she declared to the British people, "I declare before you all that my whole life whether it be long or short shall be devoted to your service and the service of our great imperial family to which we all belong" (21st Birthday Speech) she has always done what she believed was right and what made sense rather than what was expected of her. This speech should been seen as no different. As Her Majesty continues to reign, three years away from becoming the longest reigning Monarch in British History after Queen Victoria, the world will not see any decrease in the influence of Queen Elizabeth II as a leader of fifty-three nations and figure of change in many more.

Works Cited

Hardman, Robert. *Her Majesty: Queen Elizabeth II and Her Court.* New York: Pegasus, 2012. Print.

Her Majesty Queen Elizabeth Alexandra Mary Windsor. "*21st Birthday Speech.*" YouTube, 20 Sept. 2012. Web 5 Feb. 2009.

Her Majesty Queen Elizabeth Alexandra Mary Windsor. "*Dublin Cas tle Speech.*" YouTube, 12 Sept. 2012. Web. 19 May 2010.

Her Majesty Queen Elizabeth Alexandra Mary Windsor. "*Diana, Prin cess of Wales Tribute.*" YouTube, 16 Sept. 2012. Web. 2 January 2007.

Editorial Team's Note

In this essay, Matthew Armelli demonstrates the importance of ethos and pathos in the speeches of Queen Elizabeth, showing how she uses particular strategies in order to build rapport with her audience. In the cases addressed, it was important for Queen Elizabeth to use her words to build peaceful relations with the Irish, thus demonstrating the importance of careful rhetorical choices within the public and political realm. How do other political figures use ethos and pathos to connect with their audiences? What could potentially go wrong if these public figures make unwise rhetorical choices? When watching or listening to speeches by political leaders, think about who they are addressing and what bridges they are attempting to build. How does language work to connect rhetors and audiences? How might you utilize similar strategies in your own work in order to make connections with your audience?

Reflective Narrative Award

Why Ain't You Just Say That?

Makkah Beasley

Writer's Reflection

Starting my reflection was difficult—hell, even starting the paper was difficult. I thought I was going to be writing to a nameless, faceless cloud before I started thinking about audience. My English classes in high school always gave us a general understanding of Audience and didn't go into depth or make it a personal aspect of writing. It's interesting that I didn't get this kind of education until college, but better late than never I suppose...as I looked around the room analyzing my class.

I was sitting in a room—for lack of a more witty turn of phrase, white people—with the exception of one other African American on the other side of the room. The ratio I'm implying is obvious. That's when I first identified which of my "Englishes" to write about. It is very likely that the majority of my audience would be somewhat familiar with slang but perhaps less familiar with how slang is used by someone in my particular shoes. So what do my shoes look like?

I grew up in a multitude of places, sometimes at inner city apartments of Cincinnati, others were near suburbia. Very interesting concept that all my life I have always been near suburbs but never actually lived there. My multiple living locations, they have greatly shaped who I am. Some of my time was solely with white and black people who spoke "proper" English, and the other time was spent with black people who either wet themselves laughing when I put --*ing* endings on words or be entirely confused when I flexed my extensive vocabulary wings. For example depending on where I am and who I am around—if I were joking with a friend, I might say "Not you gon' take my money and don't say thank you." Or "I like how you're the kind of friend that's liable to take my cash and leave me for dead."

See what I mean? As long as I can remember there have been two sides of my language, however I didn't come to this realization before writing this paper. It's almost like being bi-lingual since "standard" English in America is almost completely different from African American slang. But why is slang different? I asked myself this question for a long time. My conclusion: the culture. African American slang has been shaped by African American culture, which is why the experiences and people that indirectly taught me how to speak it vary depending on where that person came from.

But it's not exactly something I can concretely explain and express my thoughts on, because all of my opinions are not formulated yet. Which made writing this paper such a challenge. Not to mention that African American culture is so far extended in history that it would take a much long paper for me to express ALL of my opinions on the topic, but that's not the point of this paper. In a sense, it's about me. How do I use slang? Why do I use it? And what does it mean to me? It is my hope that I am successful in answering these questions for anyone who reads this paper. And it is also my hope that I continue to learn more about myself in the process.

◆ ◆ ◆

The identity of an African American can have more versatility than most people may think. For example, the way we talk. And in order for me to fully get my point across, I'm afraid I have to take us back to a dark time in American history that white people generally are uncomfortable with talking about: the days of the plantations. So if your white... clench your butt cheeks together tight and keep reading, I promise not to make you feel too guilty as we talk about slavery. Yes slavery; a familiar topic and it just so happens to be where African American slang began. Prior to coming to America, most Africans had limited or no knowledge of the English language and were only fluent in their various native dialects. It was forbidden for a slave to be formally educated or speak any other language other than English, and the little English they did learn, could be considered "broken" I suppose. It was full of mispronunciations and even some newly created words.

Thus, slang continued to be spoken amongst black people in America for centuries as slavery continued, slang unrelenting evolved into somewhat of a new language altogether, past down from generation to generation. However things have changed, we have education now...no child gets left behind and all that jazz. So if black people know how to speak "properly" then why do some still choose to make various English teachers' ears bleed? Simple, because slang is a part of an identity, in essence it means you're cool, your included; you belong with your peers. This is why a black person not speaking slang might seem "stuck up" or arrogant to someone that does; it might subtlety imply that they are trying to present themselves as superior in knowledge. But as I already tried to point out in the previous paragraph: slang is not a representation of a lack of intelligence. Anyone can be stupid, whether they speak slang or not. But regardless, for some it's no different than having an accent, and for others like me it's more of a choice.

There is really no such thing as a generic black person, everyone is different. We come in all kinds of shapes, shades, and personalities with just as much diversity in our use of language and word choice. Of course I cannot speak for my entire race, but I can speak for myself and my own experiences. My mother grew up similar to the way I did: surrounded by others that spoke "proper" English instead of the slang that you can hear being spoken in the inner city. Not surprisingly most of these people speaking "the right way" were Caucasian. As I continue to overuse the use "quotes" repeatedly in this paper with certain words and phrases, I can hear the most of them playing in my head directly from my memory.

You might think that these critics of my speech were white people, but irony doesn't work that way. Yes, 100% of the citizen or raised eyebrows I have ever received were from fellow black people. My hypothesis is that they are merely puzzled. They do not understand why I pronounce the -ing endings and neglect to use "ain't" – which by the way is kind of a synonym for "not", and other words that Webster is not familiar with. It's perplexing that I would choose to use the word... perplexing. Most black people that I know can turn slang on and off like a switch; they choose when and where they speak slang. This was exactly my situation that was so natural that it almost wasn't a choice but a reflex.

When I would go out with my black friends I spoke slang like they did. And when I went with my white friends I would pronounce those –ing endings I was talking about. You might be wondering what would happen if I were to meet both friends at the same time... this has never happened to me personally because there has almost always been such a clear division and distinction between my two groups of friends, where my flexible personality met somewhere in the middle. However the most relevant memory I can dig up involves my slang speaking older cousin and my non-slang speaking older sister. The incident was on a sunny day, with at irrelevant date and time...

My sister and I were talking about a television show that we both deeply enjoy. I asked my sister if there were going to be new episodes soon and she told me that the show was in syndication. In mid conversation my cousin interrupted my sister – a normal thing in my family, and said "What?" Allahna and I turned to her with confused expressions and said "What?" (Such an articulate bunch we are). "What did you just say?" Ronnetta motioned to my sister. Allahna thought for a moment and slowly said: "Syndication?" "Yes!" Ronetta said nodding. "It's where individual stations buy programs outside of the network system so they only show re-runs, and there are no new episodes." Allahna said with a smile, she was clearly amused by our cousin's animated facial expressions. "Oh," Ronnetta said looking less confused. "Why ain't you just say that then?" My sister and I both laughed. "I don't know." Allahna said still chuckling. My cousin was smiling too but she rolled her eyes and we all started talking about something else. Looking back on that situation, I hope we didn't hurt Ronnetta's feelings when we laughed at what she said. The humor was really only in the way she spoke. You have to know that I am understating her vibrant personality when I say that she is "animated". It makes for some interesting holidays and family events.

But the point is not that my cousin didn't know what "syndication" meant (loads of people don't), the point is that she thought it was completely unnecessary to use the word. Which might be way she relies on slang more than I do myself, I love to learn new words and use them at every opportunity I can. As a matter of fact I have used something this paper already! Regardless of the reasons ofothers, I speak slang by choice. Many times I considered if I was just trying to fit in and if I was being true to myself or not. But I think it goes further than that. I speak slang when I am with close friends and relatives who also do not speak slang any other time...well more or less, sometimes I unconsciously flip flop between the two.

But it's about a form of acceptance, a cultural differentiation that makes me feel relaxed and informal. I'm sure many would agree that African American slang is different than how we think of the "normal" standard of English. Several of the words are similar to "standard" words but they are broken up, mispronounced or new words are just created all together. And yet it is still English, a type of

English at least. And it has its uses, although many of the made up words I could do without just because of the pure nonsense of some of it. For example, there are many contractions in English like "it's" and "you're" but none for "you all" or "you guys", and thus "yall" was born... very necessary in many circumstances, not to mention it just rolls off the tongue. However "skep" is seems that it is implying that something is skeptical but if you guessed that, you would be wrong. It actually means that something is "messed up" or "bad".

For example if I saw you steal a cookie from the store I might say "man that was skep". It's confusing and I would like to know who made up the word that has recently been added to the urban dictionary so that I can give him or her piece of my mind... While I do frown on some aspects, I like slang on the whole because of what it means now more so than where it came from. Furthermore I hope you have enjoyed this journey through deteriorating precious minutes of your time reading the ramblings of an "Oreo" young woman (black on the outside, white on the inside). Nevertheless, I have been using slang less and less recently because college seems to call for bigger vocabulary words to explore and have fun with, but that doesn't mean that I might not meet some new people that inspire me to talk how I be doin'.

Editorial Team's Note

In this award-winning reflective narrative, Makkah Beasley describes how her identity as a black woman is tied up in the language she uses. She recognizes how language—and specific dialects—have long, sometimes tragic, histories, prompting the reader to consider how ways of speaking are entwined with our identities. As Beasley reflects on how language is inevitably tied to power, she explains how she moves back and forth between "African-American slang" and "proper English." This is what literacy scholars call *code switching*, and it's something we all do. Think about how differently you may speak to your friends, your parents, and your teachers. As you read, consider moments where you've code switched and why. Were you speaking "proper English"? Is "proper English" always the best way to communicate to particular audience?

Literary Analysis Award

Feminist Fears: The Cultural and Historical Context
of *The Handmaid's Tale*

Maria Grosso

Writer's Reflection

For my cultural and historical analysis paper, I wrote about how the Republic of Gilead in *The Handmaid's Tale* showed the backlash against feminism in the 1980s and how a literal interpretation of religious texts can lead to the oppression of women. I chose to write about that because it was a theme that caught my attention immediately while I was reading. It also is something that genuinely interests me because I grew up Roman Catholic but don't agree with much of the literal interpretation of the Bible that characterizes Catholicism. I believe that much of what is written in the Bible can be interpreted the wrong way, causing women and other minority groups to be treated unfairly. Therefore, *The Handmaid's Tale* really seemed to help me gather my own thoughts and beliefs together. It also inspired me to think further about how I can integrate my religious views with what I believe is right—something that I have always struggled with.

In terms of my paper, I felt that I did a pretty good job providing enough background for my topic and how it related to the text. It was actually very surprising how well quotes from my outside sources as well as quotes from *The Handmaid's Tale* meshed together in my paper. I know that I would not have been able to do this as effectively if I hadn't worked so hard on my annotated bibliography. Because of this, I now understand more than ever that writing is a process that takes time. Before this paper, I thought that if I paid attention in class, came up with an idea, and executed it, I would produce a quality paper. Now I know that writing is much more complicated than that and involves baby steps. I learned that it is ok to throw ideas out, start over, and drastically revise. However, even more importantly than that, I learned how crucial it is to understand a text in its cultural and historical context. Without thoroughly understanding where an author is coming from or in what time period they are writing, part of the story is missing. From now on, I will try to situate the texts I read in a larger context in order to get the most information out of them. This is a new concept for me, but I know it will be helpful in future courses I take here at Miami University as well as when I graduate.

◆ ◆ ◆

Imagine living with the constant fear that decades worth of progress might be taken away. The story told in Margaret Atwood's *The Handmaid's Tale* brings life to such fears that feminists had during the 1980s. These fears arose because the 1980s was a time in which religious conservatives gained power and caused many to think that gains women had made in previous decades, such as freedoms of sexual expression, access to contraception, and non-traditional gender roles, would be reversed. *The Handmaid's Tale*, therefore, mirrors this backlash against the rise of feminism and the sexual revolution of the 1960s and 1970s. In the novel, the Republic of Gilead is a society that shows the consequences of a complete reversal of women's rights based on literal interpretations of Biblical teachings. Women are no longer allowed to read, write, or think for themselves; instead, their sole purpose is to reproduce. Through the narration of Offred, a handmaid in the novel, I believe Margaret Atwood argued that the rise in Christian fundamentalists during the 1980s undermined some of the progress women had recently gained and showed that a literal interpretation of the Bible can lead to the oppression of women.

First, I believe Margaret Atwood showed that Christian fundamentalists during the 1980s undermined some of the progress women had recently gained through the creation of the Republic of Gilead in her novel. However, this is hard to understand without the historical context of and leading up to the 1980s. The 1980s was a time when "church-based groups were increasingly involved in debates over reproductive and family issues" (Rindfuss et al. 493). Specifically, religious conservatives took stances that strongly opposed the sexual revolution of the 1960s and 1970s, which was characterized by "widespread access to contraception, the legalization of abortion, and more non-traditional gender roles" (Rindfuss et al. 502). While feminists of the time thought that the sexual revolution helped women gain confidence and freedom in their sexuality, many religious groups were opposed and wanted a return to traditional gender roles and family life. Therefore, with the rise in fundamentalist and conservative Christians in the 1980s, feminists obviously had fears that everything they worked for would be undone. Margaret Atwood's creation of the Republic of Gilead in *The Handmaid's Tale* was a way that made those fears and insecurities a reality on paper.

In that fictional reality, women are used only as objects for procreation. This is shown in the text when Offred says, "We are for breeding purposes . . . There is supposed to be nothing entertaining about us, no room is to be permitted for the flowering of secret lusts; no special favors are to be wheedled, by them or us, there are to be no toeholds for love. We are two-legged wombs, that's all sacred vessels, ambulatory chalices" (Atwood 136). Through this quote, Offred explains that her only worth is through being an object for reproduction. This is diametrically opposed to how she viewed herself and her body before the religious extremists created Gilead in the novel. This is shown in the novel when she says, "I used to think of my body as an instrument, of pleasure, or a means of transportation, or an implement for the accomplishment of my will. I could use it to run, push buttons of one sort or another, make things happen. There were limits, but my body was nevertheless lithe, single, solid, one with me" (Atwood 73). This quote shows that she could experience sexual pleasures, go where she wanted, and do all of what she desired before Gilead. The contrast between these two quotes, in my opinion, shows that Margaret Atwood argued that women had lost a sense of confidence and respect for their bodies with the new rise of religious conservatives during the 1980s. Although women's rights in reality were not restricted in exactly the same ways or with the severity that they were in Gilead, the 1980s was still "a time of substantial social and political upheaval that saw the renewed vigor of the antiabortion movement and increasing public discourse about sexual behavior" (Rindfuss et al. 502). This created a lot of anxiety and a loss of momentum for feminists who fought for more sexual freedom, which undoubtedly undermined at least some of their progress. Gilead is a great representation of all of the worst fears of feminists at the time because all sexual freedom and confidence for women was taken away.

In addition to showing that the rise in Christian fundamentalists during the 1980s undermined progress towards equality and freedom of expression for women, Margaret Atwood also showed that a literal interpretation of the Bible can lead to oppression. In the 1980s, there was a large rise in Christian fundamentalists, people who stress that the Bible should be interpreted literally as a historical record and as guidance for faith and morals. Through the Republic of Gilead, Atwood showed how this interpretation of scripture can lead to inequality and even oppression of women. Gilead's basis of literal Biblical teachings can be seen from the following quote from Offred: "It's the usual story, the usual stories. God to Adam, God to Noah. *Be fruitful and multiply, and replenish the earth.* Then comes the moldy old Rachel and Leah stuff we had drummed into us at the Center. *Give me children, or else I die. Am I in God's stead, who hath withheld from thee the fruit of the womb? Behold my maid Bilhah. She shall bear upon my knees, that I may also have children by her*" (Atwood 88). Through this quote, it is obvious that the Bible is the justification and reason that women are only used for reproductive purposes in Gilead. If a woman is too old to have children or thought to be infertile in Gilead, then a handmaid is used to have children in her place. This is Offred's role in the story as a handmaid as well as the basis for Gilead in general due to declining birth rates. Offred also says in the novel that "not every Commander had a Handmaid: some of their Wives have children. *From each,* says the slogan, *according to her ability; to each according to his needs.* ... It was from the Bible, or so they said" (Atwood 117). This quote shows that women in the novel are used by men and for men. Although these quotes show that Gilead was based off of literal interpretations of the Bible, there are deeper reasons as to why a literal interpretation of scripture leads to the oppression of women.

There are multiple reasons why a literal interpretation of scripture can lead to the oppression of women, but Atwood demonstrated points based in sociology and in the language of scripture. Obviously the details are far more complicated and overreaching than this paper can cover, but overall the idea is that religious ideas and values permeate society just like any other social institution. One sociologist said it very eloquently when she said that "religious worldviews and justifications of social conduct are two sides of the same coin" (Shaffer 792). This applies directly to the text and its historical context because at the time that *The Handmaid's Tale* was written, as stated previously in this paper, Christian fundamentalists and conservatives were increasing in prominence. By creating the Republic of Gilead, Margaret Atwood addressed the fact that society as a whole was affected by that rise. I believe she specifically focused on Gilead's control of gender roles and sexuality because "both the Hebrew Bible and the New Testament portray God in overwhelmingly masculine terms, such as Lord, King, Father, Judge, Mighty Warrior, and so on" (Burns 424). These masculine concepts of the divine, no doubt, contributed to the justification of the subjugation of women in the text as well as in society in the 1980s. Therefore, it is easy to see that a literal interpretation of scripture can have a negative impact on women because a society's interpretation of and reaction to a text with masculine bias can and does affect societies who take it literally.

The Handmaid's Tale was a nightmare made into fictional reality for any feminist in the 1980s. Through her creation of the Republic of Gilead, Margaret Atwood expressed that the rise in Christian fundamentalism during that time undermined some of the progress women had recently gained from the recent sexual revolution of the 1960s and 1970s. She also showed that a literal interpretation of the Bible can lead to the oppression of women. Through these, I believe she argues that religious interpretations and expressions should be used with caution. In the United States, a country celebrated for its diversity and acceptance of people from multiple backgrounds, beliefs, and worldviews, people need to be aware of the fact that religion has played, is playing, and will continue to play "surprisingly strong private, spiritual, and public roles" (Marry 18). Due to this, it is important that people who have strong beliefs try their best to not impose their beliefs on others. Although history has provided many examples of oppression based on extremist views, it is easy to get caught up in present circumstances. Atwood wrote in the historical notes section of the novel the following that sums up what I believe she is trying to say: "As all historians know, the past is a great darkness, and filled with echoes. Voices may reach us from it; but what they say to us is imbued with the obscurity of the matrix out of which they come; and, try as we may, we cannot always decipher them precisely in the clearer light of our own day" (Atwood 311). Therefore, I believe that Margaret Atwood highly encourages her audience to be mindful of others and to not take any interpretation of religion or text to an extreme in order to avoid inequity of people or groups in society.

Works Cited

Atwood, Margaret. *The Handmaid's Tale*. New York: Anchor Books, 1998. Print.

Burns, Elizabeth D. "Is There A Distinctively Feminist Philosophy Of Religion?" *Philosophy Compass* 7.6 (2012): 422-435. *Philosopher's Index*. Web. 16 Oct. 2012.

Marry, Martin E. "Transpositions: American Religion in the 1980s." *Annals of the American Academy of Political & Social Science* 480. (1985): 11-23. *America: History & Life*. Web. 16 Oct. 2012

Rindfuss, Ronald R. et al. "The Changing Impact of Religion on the Sexual and Contraceptive Behavior of Adolescent Women in the United States." *Journal of Marriage & Family* 60.2 (1998): 493-504. *SocINDEX with Full Text*. Web. 16 Oct. 2012.

Shaffer, Leigh S. "Religion as a Large-Scale Justification System: Does the Justification Hypothesis Explain Animistic Attribution?" *Theory & Psychology* 18.6 (2008): 779-799. *Academic Search Complete*. Web. 16 Oct. 2012.

Editorial Team's Note

In her literary analysis of Margaret Atwood's *The Handmaid's Tale*, Maria Grosso demonstrates the fear and anxiety surrounding the rise of Christian fundamentalism in 1980s America through analyzing the rules and regulations of the society found in Atwood's text. Grosso makes an effective argument through balancing historical and cultural background information with close analysis of the novel. When reading, pay close attention to how Grosso's paragraphs build upon each other. She begins by introducing her argument and providing background information, and then uses that information to examine Atwood's text. And then, as she concludes her essay, she does not just restate everything that she's already said in the essay, but instead explores the larger implications of Atwood's work for American society today. As you write your own essay, consider how you might use your research to inform your own close readings and analysis of your source text. What information is needed for your audience to be able to follow your argument? What information can be left out? What might the larger implications of your argument be?

Public Research-Based Argument Award

The Importance of a Musical Education
Daniella Conti

Writer's Reflection

At first, this paper seemed a little daunting. It was and still is the largest and most extensively researched paper I have ever written. But I was interested in my topic, I love music and I play an instrument and to have those two passions combined for my argument gave me strong motivation to research and write a persuasive paper.

Not being familiar with the format or the research aspect of the paper was challenging. I found that the majority of the criticisms of my writing were that of not analyzing and explaining my sources enough. In most of my writing, I would insert a quote and not tie it into my argument. Because I was interested in my topic and have my own opinions about it, I would often add my own opinions that had no credible research to back them up. For instance, I wrote in my initial draft that instruments could cost upwards of five hundred dollars. I didn't find this information in my research; it was my own inferences and experiences. The reason I changed these aspects of my paper was because I realized that I wasn't writing the paper for my own benefit, the paper was crafted to persuade others that musical education is beneficial to children's learning processes. If someone reads the paper and thinks that something is not convincing, then it should be changed, that was my thought process.

◆ ◆ ◆

Dear PTO of Rosedale Elementary,

This proposal addresses the benefits of musical training on the brain and cognitive development of young children. These skills that are learned through musical training help children succeed in the classroom. This information is then used to support the music education system within elementary schools. It covers the fact that musical training is easier and more cost effective for both the parent and child if it is found within the school setting. However, funding for musical education is rapidly decreasing. Most of the funds allocated to the elementary schools are being divided unevenly among the different departments. More money is awarded to those subjects that are covered in standardized testing and deemed more important than learning to play a musical instrument. I also learned how to play an instrument as a child and continue to use the skills I learned in that training in my everyday life.

Background and Goals

For many elementary school students, entrance into the band has become a rite of passage. Every year in schools all across the nation students wait eagerly for their chance to begin learning an instrument of their choice. There is an instant attraction for some towards creating music. For those few it is not only a class or an extracurricular activity, but also a passion that can be developed and enjoyed for the rest of their lives. What if this seemingly inconsequential pastime has other benefits than fulfilling the required credit hours? It has been long thought that learning to play a musical instrument increases one's intelligence. Current scientific studies show that this kind of thinking is correct, especially for those children who begin their musical training at a young age. "During the brain's early years, neural connections are being made at a rapid rate" David Sousa, an international consultant in educational neuroscience wrote in the American Association of School Administrators' *The School Administrator* (Sousa). The skills required to create music with an instrument "...challenges the brain in new ways" (Sousa). These skills can help children perform better in the classroom and have an over all successful educational career. Skills such as learning to differentiate between different tonal sounds and developing fine motor skills in order to physically play the actual instrument (Sousa).

Unfortunately, this kind of education is not available to children of all demographics and social groups. Music lessons are expensive and time consuming, involving parents or guardians to take time from their workdays and bring the child to the lesson. Even buying the instrument can become an obstacle because most classical instruments cost hundreds of dollars. Which is where the public education system should step in. Music education programs in elementary schools are disappearing. "As budgets are cut nationwide, the funding for non-tested subjects are affected first, because the majority of resources are directed at the areas that are tested for accountability" Christina Schneider states in her article, "Measuring Student Achievement In The Future Based on Lessons From the Past: the NAEP Arts Assessment", in *Music Educator's Journal* (Schneider 56-61). Because musical progress or performance is difficult to measure it cannot be tested in the traditional means. As an administrator, one will not want to give a portion of their funds to music education if they see that test scores are low in math or science because these subjects are on found in standardized tests. But if music education is helping children to be successful in the classroom, administrative teams in the school system should be encouraging the programs, not depleting their resources.

However, this thought process is understandable from the perspective of the school's administrative staff. Standardized test scores are important for schools to increase their enrollment and government funding. Who is left to address this important but often forgotten aspect of education? A great majority of changes made in the schooling system are brought about by the parents of the children, who will always have the children's best interest at heart. Instead of a parent having to find private lessons for the child, the music education programs provide a safe learning environment for a fraction of the cost of private instruction. It is also convenient for the parents to have the musical instruction at the school so that there is not a transportation issue. It is to every family's best advantage to advocate for musical education in schools.

Support for Musical Education

Musical education is not just an extra class taken to make up for a requirement; it helps build a foundation of learning for the child's entire life.

> When you practice an instrument every day it gives you discipline. When you play in an ensemble you learn to work with other people. When you learn to read music you're learning a new language and every language you learn makes the next one you learn easier. (Brown)

Roger Brown President of Berklee College of Music gives his support for musical education in his interview with ArtistsHouseMusic.org by stating that these classes give children a chance to learn new skills to help them succeed in other areas of life. The classroom is one of the most important of these areas as well as most observed. A child who has learned the skills needed to play an instrument has also developed different neurological advances. Especially skills needed for reading and reading comprehension. "Phonological awareness relates to the ability to aurally discriminate between sounds or to be sensitive to all units of sound" as a music student must learn to determine between two different notes (Hansen and Bernstorf). This relates to exercises in rhyming often used in a classroom setting that teaches children to understand the relationship between rhyming pairs and the different syllables of a word.

Phonemic awareness deals with a child's ability to associate certain groupings of letters in a word with sounds, these are called "phonemes—the smallest units of oral language" (Hansen and Bernstorf). As a music student, a child will learn to recognize a musical note to mean a certain sound or tone. This neurological connection is important when that same child goes to read a passage from a book, the action uses the same connection, which has already been made or solidified by the musical training.

Another essential skill gathered through musical training is that of fluency. A musical student learns fluency when reading sheet music and having to play one note while looking ahead at what the next will be. This prepares and aids a child in reading aloud. This is also the culmination of all the other skills as addressed prior. In order to achieve fluency in both musical training and reading instruction, a student must engage the skills of phonological and phonemic awareness, as well as many other skills.

However, reading skills are not the only form of neurological advancements made by musical training. Mathematic and numeracy skills are developed when learning to play a musical instrument.

> Counting is fundamental to music because one must count beats, count rests and count how long to hold notes. Music students use geometry to remember the correct finger positions for notes or chords on instruments. Reading music requires an understanding of ratios and proportions so that whole notes are held longer than half notes. (Sousa)

Learning to use numbers in a setting other than the traditional math class introduces children to mathematics in fun and new ways. A child who is taking music lessons can apply what they learned in band class that day to their math lesson as well. When the students begin to notice that the skills he or she has learned are not just to achieve a high score on a test, learning comes full circle.

Proposed Plan

As the PTO of the school, many decisions rely on the support you as a group can give. An administrative team may have to answer to a higher authority cannot act as freely as the PTO can. Even though petitions and interviews with higher-ranking administrators can be arranged, the allocation of funds within the school system is a complicated process and to change it, is even more daunting. I propose that the PTO takes charge of a supplementary fund for musical education. Create a sub-committee that works with the music students and band director to organize fundraisers. It would be most efficient to have the sub-committee comprised of parents who have children taking music classes or are in the school's band so that they have a direct connection for current information.

This subcommittee should then work with both the administrative staff of the school and the students to try and create ways of raising funds for the musical education program. For example, the PTO could host a benefit or a gala and accept donations. Or the sub-committee could involve the music students and put on a concert, with the proceeds from the tickets going towards the musical education program.

It would also become the duty of the subcommittee to explain the importance of this musical education program. There should be more extensive information nights for parents of children interested in becoming involved in the program. Some of the topics covered might involve how musical education enables brain development and advanced learning processes. Perhaps this more formal information can go with the team building aspects of playing in a band and the disciplinary life style a music student needs to adopt. These information nights should also include input from the music teachers as well as current students. This way the children and the parents can have a connection to the program on a more personal level.

The final part of the proposal would be the installation of a rental system for musical instruments. Buying a musical instrument is expensive, and if a child wants to try and learn how to play but decides after a few months that it is not for him or her, then the money spent on the instrument is a waste. The implementation of a rental system would allow for parents of students try learning a musical instrument without the restriction of having to purchase an instrument. This could also lead to a student being able to learn multiple instruments more easily and cost efficiently than without the rental system. To begin the system, the PTO could have a fundraiser and buy a few different instruments, building up the school's own reserve. Another option could be to petition a local music store to donate a few instruments to the school.

Criticism

Even though there have been multiple studies performed to complete our understanding of the connection between the human brain and music, there is still much more to question and answer. The brain is a complicated organ and the way that it interacts with music creates more questions than gives answers.

However, the most predominant criticism is that of nature vs. nurture. This is the idea that it is not the musical training that enhances a child's ability to learn and succeed in the classroom, but the home environment. It may well be that a student who is learning to play an instrument was encouraged to do so by a parent. It also might happen that this parent was able to start their child's brain development early, but reading to them every night, or playing interactive games when them before they could even speak.

A study that David Sousa uses in his article, "How the Arts Develop the Young Brain" proves otherwise. The study involved taking a group of adults, who were not musicians, and training them over a period of a few weeks to pick out certain tonal changes in sounds. After the initial training time, the group of adults showed a higher performance level in the auditory processing area of their brains (Sousa). This one study shows that it is the training and not the mental capacity that improves the brain's ability to learn. It also provides support for musical training, not just in young children, for all people interested in improving cognitive development.

Conclusion

The scientific studies, facts, and statistics all lead back to the benefits of musical training on a child's developing neurological processes. This is important for a student's general development within the classroom. These skills that the students develop in conjunction with musical training involve reading and reading comprehension as well as mathematical subjects and numeracy. However, musical training goes beyond classroom development and can also form the student's character. Learning to play with a group of other instruments teaches children how to work within a group and practicing the instrument daily teaches discipline and the importance of dedicating time to a project.

There is a fair amount of studies on the topic of the effects of musical training and research even continues to develop. It is difficult to measure and study the development of the brain because so little is understood about it. It is important to continue observing how musical training effects not only the brain's development, in regards to children, but also affects their character. I believe that this is another important factor that is not as well researched, however, this could tie into the nature vs. nurture criticism. This criticism has been disproved through research, but still remains an issue among experts when discussing the advantages of a musical education. The fact remains, though, that musical education is highly beneficial to a child's cognitive and social development. Even if these facts are disregarded, learning to play a musical instrument can give a child a life long passion to pursue and continue to grow in.

Works Cited

Schlaug, Gottfried, Andrea Norton, Katie Overy, and Ellen Winner. "Effects of Music Training on the Child's Brain and Cognitive Development." *Annals of the New York Academy of Science* 1060. (2006): 219-230. *Wiley Online Library*. Web. 5 Oct 2012. <http://onlinelibrary.wiley.com/doi/10.1196/annals.1360.015/full>.

Hetland, Lois. "Learning to Make Music Enhances Spatial Reasoning." *Journal of Aesthetic Education* 34.3/4 (2000): 179-238. *JSTOR*. Web. 5 Oct 2012. <http://www.jstor.org/stable/3333643?seq=2>.

Hansen, Dee, and Elaine Bernstorf. "Linking Music Learning to Reading Instruction." *Music Educators Journal* 88.5 (2002): 17. *EBSCO host*. Web. 10 Oct 2012. <http://ehis.ebscohost.com/ehost/detail?sid=6d7dc540-38e0-4db8-9cb0-40dd38999fd2@sessionmgr12&vid=1&hid=26&bdata=JnNpdGU9ZWhvc3QtbGl2ZQ==

Sousa, David A. "The School Administrator." *School Administrator.* 63.11 (2006): n. page. Web. 20 Oct. 2012. <http://www.aasa.org/SchoolAdministratorArticle.aspx?

Schneider, Christina. "Measuring Student Achievement in the Future Based on Lessons from the Past: the NAEP Arts Assessment." *Music Educators Journal* 92.2 (2005): 56-61. *EBSCOhost.* Web. 20 Oct 2012. <http://ehis.ebscohost.com/ehost/detail?sid=2f9a3c58-9424-4ea2-aa07-048f1961577c@sessionmgr10&vid=1&hid=1&bdata=JnNpdG U9ZWhvc3QtbGl2

Editorial Team's Note

Daniella Conti's award winning proposal carefully blends together thorough discussion of sources with a clear action plan of how to proceed in addressing the issue of music education. Notice how, at the outset of the proposal, Conti positions herself and her attachment to the issue. Notice, too, the ways in which Conti addresses and accounts for multiple interest levels (from students to parents) and various stakeholders (teacher and administrators). As you read this piece, consider ways in which genre expectations (i.e. the differences between proposals and traditional research essays) assist and constrain the development of your rhetorical approach and organization of ideas on the page. Also consider ways social, cultural, and economic factors influence your perception and discussion of groups with a stake in every debate. As a rhetor, how will you account for and address audiences with conflicted perspectives entrenched in tumultuous social and economic climates?

Bedford St. Martin's Digital/Multimedia Writing Award

Battle of the Rhetorics

Kendall Schwille

You can listen to this audio project on our *CCM* companion website.

Editorial Team's Note

Listen to Kendall Schwille's audio essay, featured on the *CCM* website, and consider her reflection. Schwille's engaging retelling of her Inquiry One assignment provides a useful description of how rhetoric functions in her daily life. Especially interesting in Schwille's audio essay is her use of music, sound effects, and voice intonation to narrate her compelling story. More than this, Schwille demonstrates the careful planning that goes into presenting work in a new medium. As you listen, think about the small things Schwille does to keep her project organized and interesting. When working with sound, how might you keep your listeners engaged throughout your project? How does narrating a story change without visuals?

English 109/111 Essays

Course Description

ENG 109/111

English 109/111, Composition and Rhetoric, is a writing course focused on introducing you to the concepts and practices of rhetoric. What is rhetoric? Excellent question. According to Aristotle, "Rhetoric may be defined as the faculty of observing in any given case the available means of persuasion" (*Rhetoric*). In other words, in this class you will explore how authors analyze the rhetorical situation (context, audience, author, and text) and apply logos (logic), ethos (credibility), and pathos (emotion) to their texts in order to influence the responses of readers. You will analyze the texts, both written and visual, of others, and you will use rhetorical devices to create your own persuasive texts. You will research and analyze sources concerning a topic that interests you and compose an argument based on your analysis; you will learn how to tailor your writing to fit the needs and expectations of specific audiences; and you will remediate (that is, transform) a text from one form into another. English 109/111 will prepare you to write effectively at the college level not only in English, but also in your other courses. As you complete each assignment, you will be asked to write reflections about your writing process and rhetorical decisions. While English 109 is meant specifically for international students whose native language is not English, the materials covered are similar to those covered in English 111.

Inquiry 1: Initial Reflection

This first Inquiry invites you to think about yourself as a rhetorician in a variety of contexts. The assignment is a startup project that asks you to write about your rhetorical experiences; you might use narrative, memoir, descriptive or deductive writing, and reflection to establish and explore your composing practices, experiences, and existing knowledges of how rhetoric works in your life. You can read examples of this kind of narrative reflection in this book: Megan Caldwell's "Words without Speech" and Brittany Dunn's, "'Tom Boy' to 'Gamer Girl'" both illustrate how you might write about yourself as a critical user of language. The main purpose of this assignment is to get you to analyze and reflect on how you have used rhetoric or how rhetoric has been used on you.

Inquiry 2: Rhetorical Analysis

In this Inquiry, you will begin to explore the rhetorical appeals and modes that authors use to communicate information to their audiences. Being able to identify authors' strategies will help you to more carefully analyze the effectiveness and validity of their work. In this assignment, you will look closely at all of the rhetorical appeals of a single public text. You will choose the primary text or texts analyzed in your writing and may be asked to examine an advertisement, film, piece of persuasive or literary prose, or traditional political speech. The examples provided here all analyze significantly different texts — from Kien Dao's examination of a recent non-fiction book to Claire McCallum's analysis of a small town in Massachusetts.

Inquiry 3: Public Issue Argument

For the third inquiry, you will be asked to take positions on topics and defend those positions publically using logical and rhetorical devices and the writing of others. Most Inquiry 3 assignments allow you to choose a public social issue about which you are genuinely passionate or curious, and utilize formal research methods to investigate and understand it more comprehensively. The essays printed here, by Olivia Grieszmer and Hunter Leachman, both illustrate how you will learn to use to use invention, inquiry, and research to approach a public argument from a local or personal perspective. This research process will enable you to develop a sophisticated position in response to a public issue, and finally, construct an informed, ethical public argument. An important aspect of this Inquiry is learning to use the intellectual work and writing of others responsibly and effectively — through quotation, integration, and citation — in your own college work.

Inquiry 4: Remediation

In this Inquiry, you will consider how the media you use to present information and the audience that information is meant for can have a great effect on the type of rhetoric you include in a project. To do this, you will remediate a piece of writing you have done previously in the course, adapting and revising their messages for a digital medium and perhaps engaging multiple modalities. To "re-mediate" means to change the medium for a particular message; it also means that the message will change to suit the new medium. You can read about the ways in which Jake Prodoehl's message had to change when his audience and medium changed in his essay titled "Childhood Cancer: Little Patients; Little Patience," and view his work on the *CCM Online*. "Changing the medium" might mean taking a print document and making a YouTube video version for the Web or an audio version to play in iTunes or on the radio. It might mean making a PowerPoint or Prezi presentation to be delivered to class or making a slide show of still images, text, and spoken voiceover.

Inquiry 5: Final Reflection

This inquiry asks you to reflect on your semester of writing, your writing process, and on what you have learned about writing and communication. You will be asked to substantially revise your Inquiry One essay, which will serve as the lead and central piece in a portfolio of selected samples of your writing from English 111 (and perhaps other rhetorical artifacts). Read Ashley Hopes' and Maisie Laud's reflections, printed here and available on the *CCM Online*, to learn see how engaged reflection goes beyond simple narrative, but draws on specific experiences to make an argument about yourself and your writing.

Inquiry One: Initial Reflection

Words without Speech

Megan Caldwell

Writer's Reflection

Throughout writing this piece, I kept asking myself one question: How do I want my audience to interpret language from what I've said? I wanted to really use this reflection as a way to sprout some discussion, start a conversation that maybe hadn't been talked about as much or as deeply. I tried to think back over the years and find a conversation or instance in which language had possibly confused me, maybe a situation in which I'd come away from the conversation a little baffled or a little more thoughtful. At first, I started with interaction among other languages. Spoken languages, that is. I had a Japanese exchange student when I was younger, and I thought that could be a good point to bound from and discuss the conflicts regarding being notably "lost in translation". I could have even covered the idea of emotions and how they transcend vastly different languages, how there is always a human element to language regardless of what syllables are used.

Instead of either of those minor ideas, I settled on a small conversation that took place at a family funeral. I was initially attracted to the idea that as a young child I had difficulty understanding death—as most children around that age do—and language, with its expansive vocabulary and ways of expression, was unable to breach that divide. But then I remembered Bryan and all the emotions that I had felt while signing with him. Nothing was spoken, nothing used words. And yet, something distinct was memorable about that specific conversation. As soon as I started to write about it, I began to see language and the way we communicate as humans in a different light.
Language is not simply something that you just learn; you accept it as part of yourself. It defines you. I covered this idea in great depth as I began to understand the relationship a little more clearly. I've never written anything like that, and I must admit, it was really something to see it all come together. Granted, I can't take all the credit. Thanks again, Bryan. Wherever you are. Thank you for allowing me to view language, as human traits in general, in a different light.

◆ ◆ ◆

What is language to someone who is deaf? Words and syllables are a useless, white static. The meanings and connotations buried within even further removed. Most people take their ability to talk, the simple capacity to form words that can further be strung into elaborate and meaningful sentences, for granted. It is not done purposefully, but it happens. After visiting a family funeral one weekend, I began to form a new appreciation for the English language I had been raised in. I was roughly ten at the time, young and naïve in the ways of formalities regarding death. I'd complained the whole way to the funeral home, with my brother in close tow behind me regarding the whole situation. I pouted when I was forced to wear the tights Mom had picked out for me, and stomped my way around the house to show my general frustration. Erin, my best friend who lived down the street from us, had invited me to the movie theaters with her family. I begged Mom to let me go. Heck, I didn't even know the person who had died.

Apparently, or so Mom and Dad said, that was an unacceptable reason to skip the funeral proceedings; they were family, and as such, I was required to show my respect by attending.
When we arrived, I promptly made a beeline for the nearest available seat. Pierce joined me, and within seconds we'd already clicked on our gameboys, getting ready to follow up on an agreement we'd made in the car to hold a Pokémon battle via link-up cables. Mom was quick to intercept the plans. She called for us from the other side of the room and we both froze. To look at her would be admitting that we had heard her. To admit we'd heard her, however, would get us caught in a long adult talk that we might never be allowed to surface from. I chose to ignore the call and fully immerse myself in the game, with Pierce taking cues. Maybe now she'd finally take the hint that I didn't want to be here.

No such luck. Within moments she was next to us, calmly pressing the "off" button and ending our link-up session. Before I could even blurt out an annoyed response, she asked us to stand up and introduce ourselves. It really was the tone that forced me to move; she never used that kind of emphasis unless she was really mad. Maybe I had pushed the envelope a little too far.

"Hi, I'm Megan." I sounded utterly bored and uninterested. Mom shot me a glare.

"And I'm Pierce!" My brother joined in, regaining his usual happy-go-lucky personality as if the gameboy situation hadn't occurred. I'd take the heat for that later.

I looked at the person Mom had brought over to introduce. He seemed to be rather young, yet old enough to live on his own. He simply waved and smiled, reaching out to shake my hand. *Why isn't he saying anything*? I shot a quizzical look at Mom, wondering why on earth she wanted to introduce us to this person.

"This is Bryan. He's deaf—I told him you took a sign language class this summer and I thought you might want to show him what you know."

"Oh." It was the only word I could form at the moment in my shock. What could I even begin to say to that? "I'm sorry" sounded rude and out of place. There had to be something better I could start with.

Immediately, I was interested in my new friend and how they viewed the world. Was signing letters and meanings second nature to him, or did he still think about every motion he made? Did he interpret words the same way I did? And as most ten year olds would agree, after watching him sign, I desperately wanted to sign too. I wanted to have a conversation with him; I wanted to see the world from his point of view. Shyness began to take over. What if I messed up or signed something wrong? I'd look like an idiot; besides, I'd never signed to an actual deaf person before. Maybe it didn't really make a difference who I'd signed to, but it felt awkward and out of place. I couldn't remember the combinations of motions or the general alphabet very well by any means. Summer stretched away from me as I tried to remember something, anything to say. In a sense, signing just felt wrong; it wasn't my language and I felt like I was always butchering it beyond any definition of understanding.

I continued to stare at Bryan for another moment, considering how disrespectful I probably seemed in his eyes. Quickly, as if to make some sense of amends, I signed my name. He signed his back to me and smiled.

After I finished signing to him a little while later, I felt much relief and excitement. I'd carried quite a conversation with him over the whole funeral procession and what-not. We'd covered sports and school; it was rough, but I tried my best and I'm sure he saw that. It was strange, talking to him and yet not using my voice. It was language and it wasn't. It wasn't categorized by vocals, pitches, or tones, as I was used to. But it clearly was a form of communicating and of connecting. I'd always thought of language in the speaking sense. It had never occurred to me that it could also be the way someone's face lit up at a joke, the way a smile curved, or the impression a frown could make.

Language has had a huge impact on me, which has only grown as I have gotten older. It has provided me with the ability to communicate efficiently and quickly with other students and people in everyday life. I am able to dictate and learn, teach and read all with the words that I have been taught. It breathes new meaning into otherwise mundane things and provides us as humans an ability to understand and reflect. When I first met Bryan, I didn't understand him or his language. The more I began to consider the differences between the two of us, however, I realized that language is the same no matter what form. It creates a medium for reflection and response.

That's the thing about language. You don't grow up *with* it, you grow *in* it. It forms you and the way you consider situations, it molds and forms your reactions as byproducts of itself. You become a part of it entire. As soon as you learn how to articulate yourself—I mean, when you *really* speak—when you are able to get your point across by use of the words as emotions, when you know how to play with the meanings and sounds of simple syllables to your advantage, that is when you begin to clearly define yourself through application of a language, through relevance of yourself and your spoken conscious.

In the end, I learned that language is universal. It is used by everyone, regardless of how. It is human and it is something that no one can truly take away. I hope someday I can thank Bryan for teaching me that.

Editorial Team's Note

This essay does an expert job of weaving narrative and retrospection (reflection). Caldwell's essay begins with captivating first lines. Throughout it, she reveals her feelings and reactions to the situation as it unfolds. For example, she admits, "When I first met Bryan, I didn't understand him or his language." A major strength of this essay is that the writer explores a specific situation that occurred during a short, contained moment in time. From this moment, she draws from her own experience in order to give insight into language. She concludes that language isn't just speaking--it's "a medium for reflection and response." Caldwell tells a story and arrives at her own definition of language. Her succinct line about language really sums it all up--"You don't grow up *with* it, you grow up *in* it." By exploring a specific moment through narrative, and weaving in her current reflection on that past moment, Caldwell uses a story to explore and illustrate a complex point.

"Tom Boy" to "Gamer Girl"
Brittany Dunn

Writer's Reflection

Writing this paper allowed me to reflect on a part of my life that I would have never thought to look back on. After being assigned the paper, I was hesitant to even write about being an outcast in school. It had always been a private part of my past that I didn't really like thinking about. However, I decided that writing about it would help to bring closure to the matter and even help me realize some things about myself that I had never realized before.

I started out by just putting down every thought I had about the subject. I inserted specific personal experiences of mine but I erased them after thinking about how they might be too confusing. That thought changed soon after the peer review we had in class. My peers instead told me that adding these personal experiences would add more life to my story and make it more detailed. So, I reinserted those experiences and doing so made me feel like my story truly reflected the real me.

I also learned a few things about myself as a writer. I learned that I try too hard to write a perfect story the first time around and it makes me rush my storyline when more detail is needed. After realizing this, I slowed down and allowed myself to really look at my paper as a rough draft. I just let the words flow and take shape instead of forcing them onto the page. I finally found a way to relax while writing, rather than being tense about how perfect my paper should be.

By writing this paper, I really got a chance to look back on my life. I was able to channel how I felt into words and share my story with the reader. My classmates gave me great advice on how to improve my paper, and that advice really helped me make my story complete. I hope that maybe someday, someone will also get a chance to reflect on his or her life in the way I have through writing.

◆ ◆ ◆

I grew up with parents that weren't exactly the most technologically advanced people in the world. We had one or two TVs and that was about it. My parents wanted my siblings and I to go outside, hang out with friends, play with Legos, or do anything that they felt would spark creativity. They believed that the simple joys in life were more important than technology. Despite this fact, my knowledge of technology changed when my brother finally got a Nintendo 64 for Christmas after nagging and annoying my mom to buy it for months on end. At first, I was confused by how my brother and his friends thought playing these games were fun, so I had to try it out for myself. Ever since I picked up the controller and starting playing my brother's games behind his back, I became hooked on gaming.

At age five I was already pulling all nighters playing my favorite video games instead of riding bikes or playing with dolls. Naturally, my parents were a little concerned, but they didn't yet realize that it was the storyline and how the games functioned that really intrigued me. The video games I played provided a structured, detailed story that allowed me to feel like I was part of the game. It was like reading a book that allowed me to control the actions of the main character(s).

After being introduced to video games, I became interested in the game console itself. I began to wonder how game consoles understood controls and sent information about sounds and pictures from game cartridges to the T.V. So, I began reading the "System Information" guide that no one EVER reads and furthered my knowledge by exploring my game system. At one point, I completely de-shelled the Nintendo 64 (without my brother's knowledge) and started poking at parts. I was so intrigued by how game systems functioned that I soon became an expert on troubleshooting and I ended up helping my guy friends with their game console problems in elementary school.

All of this knowledge of games and game consoles labeled me as the "tom boy" or the "nerd" and when I joined band, the "band geek" label got slapped on me too. I also noticed that I couldn't relate to other girls. At a young age I wasn't interested in dolls and dresses and as I grew a little older I wasn't interested in makeup or chasing after boys either. I spent most of my time playing video games in my basement with my guy friends and I even looked like a boy until the age of 15. I thought all girls would shun me if I tried to become friends with them and I was embarrassed and ashamed at the fact that the only thing I knew a lot about was video games.

Then finally, during my freshman year of high school, a few girls in my class tried to befriend me. As I was conversing with them,

I realized that these girls had the same interests that I did! They were also pretty and wore girly clothes, which told me that I didn't have to hide behind boyish looks just because I loved gaming and technology, I could still be myself despite all the differences I had with most females. I was relieved to finally see that gaming wasn't just a "guy thing." I could be feminine without changing any aspect of my personality.

This realization sparked a change in how I looked and interacted with others. I said goodbye to hats, wore my hair down, started wearing dresses and began to talk to all sorts of people. My circle of friends expanded and people found me likable, but I didn't have to change anything about my personality whatsoever. I was still the same old me, I just stopped hiding behind a boyish appearance. Realizing that I could be myself and still be accepted by others allowed me to make all sorts of friends and be more outgoing. I've discovered that everyone is unique and has different interests; you just have to be understanding and willing to get to know them.

To this day, not much has changed about my feelings on gaming. Just recently, I was with my friend as I was talking to the university IT services on the phone about a problem I had been having with connecting my PlayStation 3 to the Internet. I illustrated all the problems I had been having and all the things I had done to try and fix these problems. I began to engage in a conversation filled with information about encryption keys for the WPA-PSK/WPA2-PSK security and how to find the corrupted MAC address. After hanging up the phone, I noticed my friend had a very baffled look on her face. All she could say was, "Were you even speaking English?" I replied with a smile and laughed at how confused she seemed. It made me happy to know that I could be the "gamer girl" without feeling embarrassed or ashamed.

Editorial Team's Note

Dunn's essay illustrates how our literacies can shape our identities (our understanding of ourselves and how we relate to others). In this case, she describes how her knowledge of video game systems first made her an outsider but eventually became a point of pride. Through her narrative, Dunn encourages readers to consider how their own literacies impact the way they see the world. In this way, her essay is not just a story about her expertise with gaming: it makes a larger point about the relationship between knowledge, literacy, and identity. As you read, think about how she manages to accomplish this while still crafting an engaging story. How do your own literacies shape the way you understand yourself and your relationship to others?

Inquiry Two: Rhetorical Analysis

Using Rhetoric to Solve Social Problems
Kien Dao

Writer's Reflection

I have always been interested in social issues, economics and governmental systems. When I came to the United States last year, the Great Recession and its consequences captivated my attention. Recently, I read the book End This Depression Now of Paul Krugman, the American Nobel laureate in economics. So, when we were asked to do the rhetorical analysis on an issue that we were interested in, I immediately thought about this book. On this particular essay, I focused on the rhetorical methods that Paul Krugman uses to explain the situation, persuade Americans and urge them to make a change. In my opinion, it was really interesting to see how rhetoric is actually working to address and support a solution for a social problem. To the significance of the problem, I believed this work is necessary for people, especially American, to understand. As this is a long book, choosing the best parts to understand and analyze actually challenged me. However, during the process, I realized that some really awesome ideas would pop out when you literally are writing. After the peer review, one thing concerned me was about the counterargument. So, I tried to make it more reasonable. Overall, I feel I was doing the right things and satisfied the basic requirements. In the long run, I would keep refining my points and improve my quality of writing as well as my rhetoric.

◆ ◆ ◆

Today, the economic slump is one of the most noteworthy issues in the United States. After the financial crisis happened in 2007, causing economic recession, it created negative consequences both in the United States and in the world. In the United States, millions of people became unemployed. Millions of families live with debts and without houses. Companies and firms reduce investment and production because of pessimistic expectations about the future. National debt becomes one of the most controversial issues. Globally, the situation is even worse. At this time, Paul Krugman, the Nobel Prize nominee in Economics, wrote his book *End This Depression Now*. As a macroeconomist and social scientist, Paul Krugman tried to explain the roots and causations of the current depression and to provide solutions to end it.

Published during the economic depression and before the 2012 United States presidential election, this book isn't only for the purpose of doing research or providing information about a noteworthy economic event. The essential purpose of Krugman is to help reader to know and believe what are the real problems of the American economy and what is the best way to solve it. His goal is to persuade the ordinary American people. Consequently, these people would put great pressure on their representatives in governments about decision making. Due to the ambitious nature of this book, it is well-written, persuasive and strong. Through Krugman's book, one can analyze how he uses rhetorical appeals as well as what kind of effect they have on reader.

First of all, the title of the book actually has great impact on the reader from the beginning: *End this Depression Now*. We are in an economic recession which not only costs the economy trillions dollars, but also affects human's living condition now and in the future. The title appears suddenly as a strong urge to stop it. As we read it, the pictures of people without jobs, families without houses, children without education rise in our minds. All of these evoke the sense of urgency. Now we need to and must do something to end this economic depression.

This title actually makes us worry about the current condition. However, from the other view, the title itself is a strong assertion of Paul Krugman about the way out of this. How could he say "End this Depression Now"? It's because he actually has a solution for it. He knows exactly what to do to end it. Therefore, even though it's an urge, the title is also an appeasement which assuages us about current condition that we can do something about it. Two contradictory meanings of the title add to pathos appeal. These simultaneously make the reader pessimistic and optimistic about the future. Without even opening the book, Krugman captivates the reader's attention.

Not only trying to impress reader from very beginning with the informative title, the author also keeps impressing and giving reader information with the dedication page: "To the unemployed, who deserve better." As he did earlier through the title, the author depicts a gloomy picture of the American economy. Again, this time with the dedication, he gives the reader evocative and thought provoking images of economic recession. The difference is that this time, he focuses on more specific objective, the unemployed. The reader knows that the unemployed are most affected by the economic slump. This specific mention about the unemployed evokes the reader's sympathy. Moreover, as the line reads "who deserve better," he indicates that America is not doing enough for relief. The condition is worse than it's supposed to be. This is like he is criticizing the social planners, but it's also like a little hope that we could do it better. By doing this, he accuses the politicians as inadequately dealing with the current condition, while simultaneously stating that the nation is doing under it potential. From the other view, for the unemployed reader, his kindness and good intent actually encourage them and make them more optimistic. They would be very grateful to him. All of these perpetuate to his use of the pathos appeal. More importantly, through the dedication, Paul Krugman also prioritizes his goal that this book is about and for the unemployed. This adds to the ethos appeal; he gives himself credibility and reason to write this book. Rather than political identification or economic ideology, the unemployed captivate his attention and offer him incentive to do this noble work. By declaring his charitable and passionate intent, Krugman appears to be more respected and persuasive.

In the first chapter, as the author shows how terrible the things are, one can see how dexterously he coordinates logos and pathos appeals in writing. First of all, he points out the losses from the slow growth of the U.S. economy. To achieve this, he gives the definition of an economic jargon, real GDP. Although real GDP is one of the simplest terms in macroeconomic textbook, it's easy to understand why he has to explain it. As I already mentioned above, it's because the aimed audience of this book is ordinary Americans who might not have the basic knowledge of macroeconomic. However, not only using the official definition, he also uses an example to help reader actually get the insights: "Think of it as what would happen if the economic engine were firing on all cylinders but not overheating" (Krugman 14). Next, he actually starts explaining the current situation. He states that "the U.S. economy is operating about 7 percent below its potential"(Krugman 14). As the result, we're losing "$ 5 trillion, or $ 7 trillion" that we "could and should have been earned but never materialize" (Krugman 14). Numbers and statistic increase his use of logos. They actually help reader to clearly see the huge impact of the slump. Finally, over the section, it's not difficult to notice that he continuously emphasizes the combination "could and should have been." He reveals his regret for the economic crisis, and again captivates the reader's emotions.

Following his theme of dismaying picture of the economy, Paul Krugman illustrates the losses in the future. Different from the losses we experienced or are experiencing, losses in the future are not something that we can easily address. He uses statistics, examples and research to substantiate his arguments. For example, as he talks about the loss in human capital, he uses his logical reasoning to support the point. Educating and training for the future are always the top priorities of society. However, as he states, spending cut and austerity policies triggered the "laying off of some 300,00 schoolteachers"(Krugman 16). This shows his intelligence of reasoning and making supporting ideas. Because the importance of educating is one of the few issues that we all realize, his mention about it can absolutely vindicate reader. It's like he's attacking on the weakest point of the wall. As the result of perpetual unemployment, workers' skills and self-respect are going to be tremendously depreciated. He also refers the research of Lisa Kahn, an economist at Yale to back up his point: "the graduates with unlucky timing did significantly worse, not just in the few years after graduation but for their whole working lives" (Krugman 16). These examples contribute to the use of logos and ethos appeals.

Another example of using logos in this book is when Krugman explains why we are in recession and how to get out of it. To explain this sophisticated issue, he again applies the simplification method which is using a normal life story as an example. He tells a real story about a "baby sitting co-op" of 150 young couples, "who saved money on babysitters by looking after each other's children"(Krugman 26). This system works as a small and simple economy. This is exactly like the method used in many economic textbooks, economic models, which are created to describe and explain much more complicated real economy. As the story goes, eventually, the co-op got into depression because of the lack of demand. The small depression of the co-op was not solved until the economists in the group urged the board to increase the supply of coupons, which are corresponding to money in the real economy. As he points out, what we learn from this story is that "your spending is my income, and my spending is your income"(Krugman 28).

This is one of many simple lessons in economic textbooks. However, for the general American reader, this way of telling story is much more useful and better than using mathematical model.

Throughout the book, there are many times that Krugman quotes the old writings of other people and himself. We can easily notice this in the beginning of every chapter. It turns out that his use of quotes serves many purposes. First of all, he uses them as a tool to describe the current situation. When he quotes the writing of John Maynard Keynes's book written in 1930s, he wants to illustrate that the current catastrophe is not new. He also comments that "[those lines] could have been written today" (Krugman 21). Moreover, the opening quotes sometimes are used to criticize people whom he disagree with. Using Ben Bernanke's or Alan Greenspan's words, he gives the illustrations of their wrong predictions and announcements. Following those quotes, Paul Krugman always writes sarcastic comments like: "Reading those words now, one is struck by how perfectly Greenspan got it wrong" (Krugman 54). This shows how he adroitly uses both ethos and pathos appeals to obtain his purposes. Finally, through these quotes, we can realize his success of giving himself credibility. It partly comes from his quotes of famous economists such as Keynes, Milton Friedman, or Irving Fisher, who would agree with his opinions. More importantly, he gives himself credibility by quoting himself. All the lines from his blogs or his columns of NYTIMES successfully increase his position. It's like he actually knew all of these would happen and reader should have believed him. This is the best way to persuade and convince readers.

Although Paul Krugman skillfully uses the ethos appeal to increase his credibility and plausibility, it's difficult to avoid making mistakes. In my opinion, one of his mistakes might be that he explicitly announces that he is Keynesian. Throughout the book, he continuously uses Keynes's writings to back his ideas up. Plus, he also spends one section to defend Keynesians and refuses the so-called "Keynesophobia". All of these are apparently the truths. The matter is that John Maynard Keynes is one of the most controversial economists, with Karl Marx. In America, there are a lot of people, especially conservatives, who oppose him. It's always good for one to clearly identify himself. However, it could be extravagantly inefficient if he loses some readers just because of the Keynesianism, because in this book, his paramount goal is to solve the ongoing depression. The book *End This Depression Now* by Paul Krugman is an informative, relevant and ambitious book. Its primary purpose is to get the United States back on the path to fast growth again. However, economics is the young science with a history of about 300 years. Plus, as economics' nature is a social science, people's opinions vary on the ways to approach an event. As the result of these reasons, to grab attention and get support of people, the use of rhetoric is indispensable. By analyzing this book, we clearly see how adroitly the Nobel Prize winner coordinates and combines pathos, ethos and logos appeals. Above all, through this eloquent book, he expresses the message of urgency and the concerns about consequences of the economic catastrophe to people and to the world.

Work Cited
Krugman, Paul. *End this Depression Now*. 1st ed. New York: W.W. Norton & Company, Inc., 2012. Print.

Editorial Team's Note
In this rhetorical analysis for ENG 109, Kien Dao explores the rhetoric of Paul Krugman's book *End This Depression Now*. To accomplish an analysis of such a large text, Dao first situates the book, explaining the social context that the book appeared in and responded to. With the social context explained, Dao connects his analysis of the book, and its particular elements, to the context. He is not merely analyzing the rhetorical appeals of the text, how it might use logos or pathos, but how particular elements of the book are making arguments toward the social context. For example, Dao explains that the book's title uses pathos to evoke in readers who are living through the social context a sense of urgency. Additionally, Dao analyzes the pathos and logos of the writing, the use of quotes in the book, and even the author's admitted political bias. These are all important things to consider when rhetorical analyzing texts. They are also important things to consider about your own writing: what appeals do you draw upon and how do they impact your audience or the social context you are writing in,

what do your quotes argue, highlight, and/or explain, and you should consider explaining your own biases in writing a particular text.

Welcome to Sudbury
Claire McCallum

Writer's Reflection
The second inquiry is a paper that I am particularly proud of. At first I struggled choosing a topic to write about, and when I eventually chose to rhetorically analyze Sudbury I struggled once again. It seemed abstract to me to analyze a town versus a literal text, but pursuing the topic and completing the paper helped to me to better my understanding of rhetoric and realize its presence in everyday life.

The main changes I made between the first and second draft of the paper were adding more detail to better portray the quaintness of Sudbury, and going into more depth as far as my warrants as a teenage girl went. In order to strengthen my warrants, I added a paragraph about when I found out there wasn't a homecoming or other formal dances at Sudbury's high school, and included my overdramatic, devastated reaction. The detail about Sudbury helped to give the reader a better picture of the town I was analyzing, and strengthening my warrants made for a more entertaining paper and added authenticity to my analysis. To further add authenticity to my analysis, I revised the paper again and re-turned in a third draft that replaced "pathos" and "logos" with specific emotions the town appeals to with the intent to make the paper sound more like my own voice.

◆ ◆ ◆

Have you ever heard of Sudbury, Massachusetts? My guess is no, probably not. With its population of about 16,000 people and location of roughly 22 miles outside of Boston, I would say Sudbury pretty much blends in with the rest of the towns in Metro West Boston. Thus, why anyone would choose to live in Sudbury specifically, I honestly could not tell you. In fact, I would argue that the exact pathos, ethos, and logos that Sudbury appeals to when attracting its citizens is exactly what made me, a thirteen-year-old girl at the time I moved there, hate it. But first, in order to present the fairest analysis of Sudbury I can offer, let me take you back to February 22, 2007, the day I first arrived at my new so-called "home."

***

The drive from the airport into Sudbury started out exciting as I peered out the car window to catch glimpses of Boston, and was still intriguing as we began entering suburbia and drove past the beautiful, old mansions in Weston. Shortly after, though, the drive went downhill at a drastic speed. My family and I were getting increasingly closer to Sudbury, and all I had seen surrounding either side of the road for the last mile were ugly, dried out, swampy looking wetlands.

To my relief, the wetlands disappeared once we passed a sign reading "Entering SUDBURY." Replacing them were historic, colonial-looking houses with plaques next to their front doors reading a date from the 1800s signifying when they were built. Houses without plaques greeted us too, still maintaining the same architecture as the historical ones even if they were not as old. Regardless of when the houses were actually built, the transition from the ugly wetlands to the historic, and at least historic-looking, houses was welcomed. The scenery along the arrival into Sudbury appealed to pathos, as the drastic change of environment from ugly wetlands to well kept, attractive houses was meant to be pleasing. The unique, somewhat misleading environment prior to Sudbury's entrance made the historic houses more appealing, working in Sudbury's favor by drawing out it's unique features that could have gone more unnoticed had the swamps not been prominent upon arrival.

Unfortunately for Sudbury, the charm and pathos the historical architecture was meant to appeal to did not work on me. Coming from West Chester, Pennsylvania, I had already seen the same colonial-type houses before. However, leading up to them were not swamps, but breath taking views of rolling hills. The historic houses made up for the poor arrival into Sudbury, whereas in West Chester the houses were only made more beautiful because of the attractive build up to them. Most people living in the Sudbury area have never been to West Chester and therefore would not have the same comparative experience as I did, but for me, previously living in West Chester tarnished any charm that was supposed to come out of the historic environment of Sudbury.

As my family and I began driving further into town, we reached a four-way stop known as town center. We were supposed to go straight to get to our house, but my dad insisted it would be a good idea to go right and see the high school first. "The High School" is actually called Lincoln Sudbury Regional High School, LS for short, but Sudbury prides itself on its newest seventy four million dollar, 385,000 square foot school, for a mere 1,600 students, enough that "The High School" is all that needs to be said. Adding to the hype of the school, LS consistently ranks amongst the top public high schools in Massachusetts year after year.

Driving up my expectations were not let down, with LS looking more like a small college than an actual high school complete with state of the art turf athletic fields and outdoor quads for socializing. The high school, along with the rest of the Sudbury Public School system, appeals to the ethos of the town as its facilities and educational system contribute substantially to the honorable reputation Sudbury has. Additionally, many of the high schools in the neighboring towns are over twenty years old like LS used to be, further developing Sudbury's credibility by making the town with all the new bells and whistles: the town all parents now want their kids to go to school in.

Similar to how the pathos the historic environment in Sudbury appealed to did not faze me, the ethos the school systems appealed to did not either. I can understand why from a parent's perspective a new school that offers high ranking education would give Sudbury credibility and value, but to me, a 7th grader forced to leave her former home that she loved, education was the least of my worries. Add in the fact that my dad was trying to sell me on the greatness of the school a whole year and a half before I would even be going there and the ethos LS was supposed to strengthen was drastically weakened. What LS had to offer was understandably an attractive quality to a parent or a more future oriented student, but unfortunately for Sudbury I was neither of those.

After we left LS, my Dad insisted that we take one final detour and drive down Boston Post Road. I thought this was weird at first, why one particular road out of the whole town? I soon learned, though, that Boston Post Road is practically *the* road of the whole town. Being that it is the only road that is allowed to have commercial businesses, my dad told me, it is where I found everything from the grocery store, the only two good local restaurants, some smaller cafes, a TJ Maxx, and a few other random businesses. While the real reason for the all of the commercial business being on Boston Post Road had something to do it plumbing or water supply or something, Sudbury used it to its advantage by saying that it provides a prettier, more suburban environment everywhere else in town.

Once again, Sudbury used its unique environment to appeal to pathos. By not having a random McDonald's or anything of the sort in the middle of town to attract attention or people from other towns, Sudbury appears peaceful when driving through. However, once you reach Boston Post Road, there is more chaos and you are bound to run into at least one person you know, making Sudbury appear lively and more like a real town. Sudbury's unique configuration of only homes and one street of businesses appeals to the small town feel many people seek, but still has enough essential commodities to make people feel like they are not living in the middle of nowhere.

While the people living in Sudbury think their set up is the best of both worlds, I again was not in agreement with the pathos it appealed to. It is not that the pathos is inaccurate, for Sudbury does have a small town feel but still has the basics, but I did not want a small town feel. Before living in Pennsylvania I lived in Fort Wayne, Indiana, which is exactly the opposite of small town in the sense that the number of commercial businesses, strip malls, and restaurants is endless. Moving from Fort Wayne to West Chester already felt like a drastic change as West Chester had far fewer attractions, and now Sudbury, with even less than West Chester, felt like it literally had nothing to offer. There is a lot more commercialism in neighboring towns, but this was of course no help to me, as I could not drive yet. It meant I would need to ask my parents, whom at this stage in the move I wanted absolutely nothing to do with, for a ride, and therefore was no longer an option. Thus Sudbury seemed more claustrophobic than charming to me, it felt like a trap; like the most boring town my parents could have possibly chosen to live in.

Once we reached as far down Boston Post Road could take us in the Sudbury limits, my dad finally agreed that it was time to go "home." A quick ten minutes later and we were pulling into our circle driveway. An attractive house with stone and tan paneling stood before us, and for once I could not complain. It was a nice house. But it was not the house itself that appealed to logos, but what the house symbolized: all of my dad's hard work leading up to this point in his life, and the fact that he still had a job to provide for my family and I. While there may not be much to offer in Sudbury as far as entertainment, Sudbury offered a place to live that was not far from my dad's job and would allow him a reasonable commute without sacrificing the value of education my sister and I would experience if we lived closer to his work. To him, Sudbury appealed to what he valued most, education, and providing for my family, earning Sudbury enough of a reason to move to.

At the time, I was too immature and naïve to understand the logos behind moving to Sudbury. I thought that job opportunities were endless, and that my dad could have found a job closer to West Chester if he had only tried harder. I was too unaware of what was going on outside of my thirteen year old bubble of world, and was unable to see how my dad had a very valid reason for moving us after all. I now understand that he knew things about the economy that I was too young and self-centered to consider, and that him having a job at all was far more important than where we would be living to enjoy the benefits of it. The logos Sudbury appealed to did not work on me, but it was my fault, not Sudbury's.

Overall, the rhetorical strategies Sudbury used seemingly failed upon convincing me that it was a good place to live. The unsuccessfulness of Sudbury's appeals to pathos, ethos, and logos was largely because of the exigency of the argument. The fact that I was being forced to live there made it so that I was rebelling against anything and everything Sudbury had to offer. Thus, Sudbury's arguments were practically hopeless considering the timing. I was also at an age when I was unable to appreciate things like education and employment stability, further making Sudbury's arguments fail because of the time I was at in my life. Through the historical environment, strong school system, atmosphere, and location, Sudbury offers strong appeals to rhetorical strategies. However in order to be successful in making Sudbury likable they needed a more level headed, mature audience.

Editorial Team's Note

In this essay, Claire McCallum focuses her rhetorical analysis on a unique text: Sudbury, Massachusetts. While McCallum's selected text is interesting, her analysis is especially noteworthy due to its captivating style. By incorporating a narrative structure in her essay, McCallum provides vivid imagery of her move to a small town while also incorporating a savvy rhetorical analysis of the town's features. In other words, McCallum does not forfeit engaging writing for deep analysis. McCallum's essay also demonstrates the breadth of rhetoric, as she examines how businesses, streets, schools, buildings, geographical features, and so forth, communicate particular messages to certain audiences. By applying Aristotelian appeals to these features, McCallum finally argues that Sudbury failed to win her over not due to its formal features but rather because of McCallum's unique position as a teenager moving to a small town. As such, this essay demonstrates the importance of context, timing, and audience when gauging the effectiveness of texts. Considering context and audience, what might Sudbury communicate to an older audience? What do the features of a college town, such as Oxford, communicate to certain audiences?

Inquiry Three: Public Argument

Amendment 64 and the Efforts to Legalize Marijuana
in Colorado
Olivia Grieszmer

Writer's Reflection

Within this paper, my goals are to encourage citizens of Colorado to abandon their stereotypes and assumptions of marijuana, think in an economical way, become educated on the issue, and to vote in favor of Amendment 64. I believe that I have achieved these goals through providing my audience with a broad range of information while still enforcing the positive possibilities of Amendment 64. I also utilized several different mediums such as opinion columns, news articles, and blogs to better educate my audience on the issue. My argument style throughout the paper is very similar to that of Classical Oration; this is illustrated as I make a case for my argument, provide opposing opinions, and refute against them.

I take pride in how I begin my paper with the historical perception of marijuana and how that relates to the challenges that marijuana advocates face today. I chose to begin my paper this way to persuade my audience, by means of Logos, that marijuana was once a logically approved drug and it still should be today. I am also proud of my inclusion of both opinions in my paper, those for Amendment 64 and those against it. Moreover, I still showed my support for Amendment 64 and I believe that the overall paper is still persuasive. At the same time, the fact that I covered so many topics such as the history of marijuana, Amendment 64, Colorado's efforts, and how the legalization of marijuana can help the economy, may serve as a weakness for my paper too. I feel that in a persuasive paper, one should present their audience with as much information as possible so that they can make an informed decision. To address the concern of too much information, I made sure that the bulk of my paper is about Colorado's efforts to legalize marijuana and Amendment 64. I also made sure that the additional topics covered were relevant but not overpowering. In fact, the final revisions that I made to this paper included clarifying some of the statistics I used as well as rewording factual statements to be read more smoothly, specifically in my concluding paragraph. Overall, throughout my paper, I never directly tell my audience to vote in favor of Amendment 64; I simply give them a plethora of reasons to do so. This is the most effective way to form my call to action and to persuade my audience, in my opinion.

Since the legalization of marijuana has so much potential to boost the economy, I want my audience to very clearly understand how far that impact can go and what their vote on Amendment 64 means for the United States of America. When explaining this in my paper, I utilized Pathos to connect with the readers emotions' about the poor state of the economy and the rising national debt. Furthermore, the legalization and taxation of marijuana has the potential to make a significant dent in our country's deficit and that begins with the passage of Amendment 64 in Colorado.

◆ ◆ ◆

Dr. Robert L. DuPont, national drug expert and former director of the White House Special Action Office for Drug Abuse Prevention, once believed that marijuana possession should not be a crime because the penalties do not affect users as much as necessary. Since learning of marijuana's link to health problems, he has swayed his opinion and now believes that marijuana laws need to be enforced in a stronger fashion. DuPont's change of opinion mirrors societies' perceptual changes throughout the 1970s and even connects to the societal perception of marijuana today (Leepson).

Back when Dr. DuPont was speaking out in favor marijuana in general, there was also a strong national pro-marijuana movement going on. This movement was led by NORML, the National Organization for the Reform of Marijuana Laws, which was founded in 1970. The mission of NORML is "to move public opinion sufficiently to achieve the repeal of marijuana prohibition so that the responsible use of cannabis by adults is no longer subject to penalty" ("NORML"). This pro-marijuana movement, which took place between the 1960s and 1970s, was very proactive. During this movement, eleven of the fifty states passed laws decriminalizing marijuana all together. Also,

during the 1967 presidential campaign, Jimmy Carter openly supported the decriminalization of marijuana. Dr. Peter Bourne, President
Carter's advisor on drug policies, also worked closely with NORML
during his time in office. More importantly, the 1970s was a time
when "marijuana was widely perceived as a harmless social drug —
the drug of choice for young Americans, as alcohol was for their el-
ders" (Leepson). However, society's perception of marijuana began to
change and the progress of the pro-marijuana movement was slowed
significantly when Dr. Peter Bourne was replaced with Lee Dogoloff
in 1978. Dogoloff quickly eliminated the White House's emphasis on
marijuana. President Carter stopped talking about the issue of decriminalization and Dogoloff turned the White House's efforts towards
fighting teen drug abuse. Since 1978, not one state has decriminalized
marijuana (Leepson).

   Although the progress of the pro-marijuana movement was
delayed in 1978, the idea of medicinal marijuana was gaining attention in the 1970s as well. In 1972, the US Congress sited marijuana in
Schedule I of the Controlled Substances Act as a drug considered to
have no accepted medical use ("Medical"). However, the first thought
to use marijuana in a medicinal way was in the late 18th century
where early editions of American medical journals spoke highly of
hemp roots and debris for the treatment of inflamed skin and venereal
diseases. Later on, Irish doctor William O'Shaughnessy first utilized
the fumes of burning marijuana to ease the pain of rheumatism as
well as nausea in the cases of certain contractible diseases (Stack). Today, seventeen of the fifty states have legalized the medical use of
marijuana. Those in favor of medical marijuana claim that it can be a
harmless and effective treatment for symptoms of a variety of well-
known diseases, some of which do not have a cure. Examples of these
diseases include but are not limited to cancer, AIDS, multiple sclero-
sis, glaucoma, and epilepsy ("Medical").

   One of the states who have legalized medicinal marijuana is
Colorado. As of the year 2000, Medical marijuana is legal in Colorado
according to the bill signed into law by Governor Bill Ritter (Meltzer).
Specifically, Coloradoans are permitted and given a license to possess
two ounces of usable marijuana and up to six marijuana plants at
home for a total fee of $90. These medicinal marijuana prescriptions

are given by doctors who verify that patients have conditions or diseases such as cancer, glaucoma, HIV/AIDS, persistent muscle spasms, severe pain, severe nausea, seizures (Health). In this specific effort, Colorado is not alone, provided the fact that sixteen other states are also allowing the medicinal use of marijuana today. However, Colorado is the only current state adding this controversial Amendment to the ballot this November: The Colorado Marijuana Legalization Amendment, also known as Amendment 64. This amendment is being introduced as an initiated constitutional amendment ("Colorado"). The Amendment specifically states: *"Shall there be an amendment to the Colorado constitution concerning marijuana, and, in connection therewith, providing for the regulation of marijuana; permitting a person twenty-one years of age or older to consume or possess limited amounts of marijuana; providing for the licensing of cultivation facilities, product manufacturing facilities, testing facilities, and retail stores; permitting local governments to regulate or prohibit such facilities; requiring the general assembly to enact an excise tax to be levied upon wholesale sales of marijuana; requiring that the first $40 million in revenue raised annually by such tax be credited to the public school capital construction assistance fund; and requiring the general assembly to enact legislation governing the cultivation, processing, and sale of industrial hemp."* ("Colorado"). In summary, this amendment will allow the regulation or marijuana for people over the age of 21 to use recreationally and it will also provide licenses for those who want to grow, test, and sell limited amounts of marijuana. More importantly, this amendment also requires an excise tax on the selling of marijuana, and that the first $40 million dollars in revenue received from this tax will be put directly towards the public school capital construction assistance fund.

According to Meltzer, a Rasmussen poll was taken in May of 2010 which asked Colorado voters how they plan to vote on Amendment 64. The poll found that 49 percent of voters favored the legalization and taxation of marijuana, 39 percent opposed Amendment 64 altogether, and 13 percent are still undecided. Although this seems promising, there was an amendment incredibly similar to amendment 64 known as amendment 44, which attempted the same goals in 2006 and failed 61 percent to 39 percent. However, amendment 64 is stronger this time around because new regulations have been implemented. These new regulations include licensing requirements for dispensaries and the regulation of doctors who prescribe marijuana. Overall, these new regulations actually strengthen the argument for legalization (Meltzer).

Although the argument for legalization may possess more support this time around, police and Coloradoan's alike are having mixed feelings towards the issue. It is well known that keeping marijuana illegal comes at a high price. One may wonder just how high that price actually is. A study held by the Colorado Center on Law and Policy reported that Colorado police forces spend around 4.4 percent of their budgets enforcing laws that ban marijuana. In addition, 7 percent of the judicial systems budget is spent on marijuana-related cases and 2 percent of the corrections budget is spent on arrests related to marijuana. On a national level, marijuana possession is responsible for almost half of all drug-related arrests, which are over 500,000 a year. Although these percentages are small, the can amount to copious amounts of money that will be saved by amendment 64. Specifically in Colorado, almost 6 percent of all arrests are related to marijuana. Economist Chris Stiffler predicts that the legalization of small amounts of marijuana, beginning with the passage of amendment 64, will save taxpayers in Colorado $12 million a year in the beginning and eventually up to $40 million once the amendment really beings to affect the economy (Ferner).

Regardless of the promises made by proponents of amendment 64, there are still many Coloradoans who are worried about how this will affect their lives. Opponents of amendment 64 say that it will introduce Colorado a new type of crime when people from out of state or overseas come to Colorado to buy marijuana and sell it illegally elsewhere. Olson, of the County Sheriffs association, explains "We don't want Colorado to be the 'go-to place' in the world for marijuana." In response, those in favor of amendment 64 would explain that if Amendment 64 passes, it will still remain illegal for individuals to sell marijuana. Amendment 64 only allows licensed businesses to sell marijuana and as a result, illegal sales on the streets and on the black market will disappear. Just as there is no longer a black market for alcohol as there was during prohibition, illegal marijuana sales will disappear when marijuana is made legal (Ferner).

This issue, however, is much larger than just a few pros and cons. Amendment 64 is so controversial that nearly everyone has an opinion on it. Many parents around the nation oppose the legalization of marijuana because they believe that marijuana is a "gateway drug," and that it will lead to the legalization of much more damaging drugs such as methamphetamine and cocaine (Coffman). Citizen Jeff Bailey of Denver, Colorado writes to *The Denver Post* explaining his concerns that he claims no one else has mentioned. Bailey brings up the lack of a realistic way to keep marijuana away from adolescents so it does not impair their brain development. Bailey explains, "On the one hand, we as a state we are pushing hard to raise our children's academic achievement and preparedness for a successful life, and then on the other hand advocating for laws that make it easier for kids to get high and dropout. That is insanity." On the other hand, Pat Kennedy of Lakewood expresses his feelings regarding amendment 64 very sarcastically by suggesting "if [anyone] were to look at it, [they] would find that many more kids have been killed by drivers who were wearing neckties. So obviously, we should be outlawing neckties as well as marijuana." In conclusion, many citizens of Colorado are feelings extremely mixed feelings towards amendment 64 because the repercussions of passing the issue are just so uncertain (Opinion).

A vital yet unknown possibility of legalizing marijuana in Colorado is if it will improve the economy. Coloradoans can only make logical decisions based on past experience, and so far the legalization of medical marijuana has brought in more than $5 million a year in state sales taxes (Weiner). Another historical example to compare the legalization of marijuana to is to recall the benefits of ending alcohol prohibition. Making alcohol legal again has paid off and is still benefitting the United States seeing as the industry had profited $91 billion dollars in wages and almost 4 million jobs have been created. Specifically in 2008, alcohol produced nearly $40 billion in local and state revenues. Keeping in mind that prohibition ended nearly 90 years ago, the United States is still reaping those benefits today (Erb).

The drug industry, including legal and illegal drugs, is profitable market. Many people argue that keeping marijuana illegal will continue to benefit illegitimate members of society such as dealers and cartels. On the other hand, taxpayers and police forces bear the burden of chasing these illegitimate members of society who are becoming more profitable than police are (Erb). A narcotics tasks force in San Mateo, CA who has recently been seizing the commercial sale of marijuana crops explains that indoor grow operations are able to produce three crops a year, where each crop is worth about $250,000 per crop. More importantly, right now, that's $250,000 in untaxed revenue per crop. Since the United States has a current deficit of over $16 trillion, the option to add any kind of business to the tax rolls should be appealing; this is where the legalization of marijuana can contribute to the current recession of the economy. As these facts become known to the general public of the United States, the idea of a legalize-and-tax plan becomes more popular. For example, a legalize-and-tax plan is favored by 56 percent of Californians, according to the Field Poll. This is true because in California specifically has the capability to produce annual tax revenues of up to $1.4 billion on the taxation of marijuana (Katel).

On a national level, cannabis is currently the top cash crop in twelve states. If marijuana were to be legalized nationally, the United States would save $7.7 billion on prohibition costs and gain $6.2 billion on marijuana tax revenues. The United States could also potentially gain $7 billion on cannabis coffee shops, products, and industrial hemp products. All of these earnings and savings total out to a possible $20.9 billion capital gain from the marijuana industry. For those who oppose the legalization of marijuana on a national level, studies show that 80 percent of states who have legalized the medicinal use of marijuana saw a decrease in teen drug abuse from 1999 to 2006 (Clendaniel).

In summary, Harvard economist Jeffery Miron explains, ""I think the discussion should mainly be about why marijuana should be illegal. Are there good reasons to treat marijuana differently from alcohol or tobacco? Why not let people who want to smoke marijuana smoke marijuana? We let people do all sorts of crazy things legally, from bungee jumping to downhill skiing to driving on the freeway to eating quarts of Ben & Jerry's and everything else. Why is marijuana different? I don't think it is" (Graves). Marijuana has health risks less than or equal to alcohol and tobacco. The negative consequences seem to always have a positive retort, and vice versa; but studies show that consistently around 55% of Americans are in favor of legalizing marijuana (Clendaniel). Overall, if the legalization of marijuana can save the federal government as much $13.7 billion annually, who are we, as Americans, to vote against a chance at a more stable economy?

Works Cited

Clendaniel, Morgan. "The Insane Economics of Not Legalizing Mari juana In One Handy Infographic." *Co.Exist*. Co.Exist, 06 Apr. 2012. Web. 18 Oct. 2012. <http://www.fastcoexist.com/1679641/the-insane-economics-of-not-legalizing-marijuana-in-one-handy-infographic>.

Coffman, Keith, and Alex Dobuzinskis. "Opponents of Legalizing Marijuana Focus on Risk to Teens." *Reuters*. Thomson Reuters, 22 Sept. 2012. Web. 18 Oct. 2012. <http://www.reuters.com/article/2012/09/22/us-usa- marijuana-legalization-idUSBRE88L07S20120922>.

"Colorado Marijuana Legalization Initiative, Amendment 64 (2012)." *Ballotpedia*. Lucy Burns Institute, 15 Oct. 2012. Web. 18 Oct. 2012. <http://ballotpedia.org/wiki/index.php/Colorado_Marijua na_Legalization_Initiative,_Amendment_64_%282012%29>.

Erb, Kelly Phillips. "Stirring the Pot: Could Legalizing Marijuana Save the Economy?" *Forbes*. Forbes Magazine, 20 Apr. 2012. Web. 18 Oct. 2012. <http://www.forbes.com/sites/kellyphillipserb/2012/04/20 /stirring-the-pot-could-legalizing-marijuana-save-the-economy/2/>.

Ferner, Matt. "Marijuana Legalization In Colorado: From The Black Market To The Corner Store." *The Huffington Post*. TheHuffIngtonPost.com, 26 Sept. 2012. Web. 18 Oct. 2012. <http://www.huffingtonpost.com/2012/09/26/marijuana-legalization-in_n_1915649.html>.

Graves, Lucia. "How Legalizing Marijuana Could Reduce The Federal Deficit." *The Huffington Post*. TheHuffingtonPost.com, 20 Apr. 2012. Web. 18 Oct. 2012. <http://www.huffingtonpost.com/2012/04/20/how-legalizing-marijuana-could-save-137-billion_n_1441194.htm>.

Health Magazine. "Medicinal Marijuana by State." *Colorado*. Health Media Ventures, Inc., n.d. Web. 17 Oct. 2012. <http://www.health.com/health/gallery/0,,20345389_5,00.html>.

Katel, Peter. "Legalizing Marijuana." *CQ Researcher* 12 June 2009: 525-48. Web. 18 Oct. 2012.

Leepson, Marc. "Marijuana Update." *Editorial Research Reports 1982*. Vol. I. Washington: CQ Press, 1982. 105-24. *CQ Researcher*. Web. 16 Oct. 2012.

"Medical Marijuana ProCon.org." *Medical Marijuana ProCon.org*. ProCon.org, 16 Oct. 2012. Web. 17 Oct. 2012. <http://medicalmarijuana.procon.org/>.

Meltzer, Erica. "Colorado Pot Advocates Plan 2012 Legalization Push." *Colorado Daily*. Weather Data CustomWeather, Inc, 06 Nov. 2010. Web. 18 Oct. 2012. <http://www.coloradodaily.com/cu-boulder/ci_15281752>.

"NORML Foundation." *NORML: Working to Reform Marijuana Laws*. NORML Foundation, 2012. Web. 17 Oct. 2012. <http://norml.org/about/norml-foundation>.

Opinion, DP. "Amendment 64: Should Colorado Legalize Marijuana? (5 Letters)." *Denver Post Blogs*. The Denver Post, 29 Sept. 2012. Web. 18 Oct. 2012. <http://blogs.denverpost.com/eletters/2012/09/29/amendment-64-colorado-legalize-marijuana-5-letters/19543/>.

Stack, Patrick, and Claire Suddath. "Medical Marijuana." *Time*. Time, 21 Oct. 2009. Web. 17 Oct. 2012. <http://www.time.com/time/health/article/0,8599,1931247,00.html

Weiner, Rachel. "No, Mitt Romney Will Not Legalize Pot." *The Washington Post*. The Washington Post, 02 Oct. 2012. Web. 18 Oct. 2012. <http://www.washingtonpost.com/blogs/election2012/wp/2012/10/02/no-mitt-romney-will-not-legalize-pot/>.

Editorial Team's Note

In this essay, Olivia Grieszmer tackles a complex public controversy by presenting a nuanced, thorough presentation that focuses on this issue in a specific time, place, and context. By narrowing the scope of the controversy to specifically examine Amendment 64 and efforts in Colorado to legalize marijuana, Grieszmer is able to analyze the controversy in an in-depth manner and represent multiple competing sides, rather than taking a broader, more general approach that would make deep analysis impossible. Though ultimately Grieszmer offers a clear argument and position, this is not stated directly until near the end of the essay, which allows the audience to read, consider, and evaluate each point as it presented. The organization that the writer has chosen for this essay supports its purpose and adds to its rhetorical appeal. How might this essay have been presented differently? Would it be more or less effective to state the argument immediately? What situations and audiences might influence the manner in which an argument is presented?

Transportation Efficiency: Oxford, Ohio
Hunter Leachman

Writer's Reflection

When this project was assigned, I found many features of the institution that could be upgraded in order to benefit, student and faculty well-being, cut costs, and benefit the stunning environment that engulfs the red brick Colonial-style buildings that make up the campus. However, I had troubles concentrating on one area and was too broad in all of my first ideas. After coming up with three realistic plans, I decided to focus my attention on the inefficient methods of transportation at Miami.

My research consisted of credible books, articles, and journals that all went hand in hand with my proposals. The authors included professors with degrees in environmental science along with a woman who graduated not too long ago from Miami University and had written a scholarly article proposing that the institution become more bike friendly. I expanded off of environmentally friendly concepts that are already being used at the University of Colorado and Portland State University.

The peer review helped mostly because it made me realize that I organized my research paper in a manner that a scientific paper would be written; with headers and sections within the paper. This method is most likely different than what the average person would choose, but I believe that it organizes my thoughts neatly by focusing on each one of my three proposals and then explaining their impacts on the university. I truly think that I can persuade Miami into implementing these ideas to create a healthier, environmentally friendly campus.

◆ ◆ ◆

Beautiful Oxford, Ohio is the birthplace of the prestigious Miami University. The medium-sized college town is organized into a grid-like pattern in which academic, athletic and residential halls are located. Having been laid out by a man named James Heaton over 200 years ago, the small town isn't exactly a great example of the world's most modern city. Yes, there are of course cars, electricity, and running water, but those things are simply rudimentary in a twenty-first century American town. Oxford is an enjoyable place to live, but there are constantly ways to improve a community, and the main issue concerned in this paper is the unconditional urgency for cleaner and more efficient methods of transportation.

As of now, Miami's primary means of transportation include walking, driving and biking. Most underclassmen don't have cars on campus mostly because the university advises against it and there are limited free parking spaces. This turns a five minute drive from East campus to the recreation center into a thirty minute walk. As a college student, one's time is already limited, and spending twenty to thirty minutes walking *anywhere* is a hindrance that most underclassmen must face at Miami at one point or another. Similarly, the Miami Metro bus system is flawed. These bulky, inefficient machines drive around campus all day, rarely having more than five riders on board. This is a massive waste of money and energy and something needs to be done about it. That is why some alternate forms of efficient transportation around Miami's campus are an essential tactic in improving the institution.

In the 2008 College Sustainability Report Card released by the Sustainable Endowments Institute, Miami received a C+ for sustainability. Institutes that received A's included Harvard, Middlebury College, and the University of Vermont. A point to consider is that Miami is not necessarily a polluted, anti-green campus. Miami University has made small steps in the past to encourage environmentally friendly practices such as the promotion of bicycling in 2006, the campus transportation study in 2008, and the Miami Circulation Plan of 2011. In the latter of these movements, a document from the president's office entitled "Miami University Sustainability Commitments and Goals" mentions the following two goals, among many others:

1. "Because sustainability comes not only through what we do, but how we invest our money, Miami University and the Miami University Foundation will work to bring more transparency and social responsibility to investment decisions."

2. "We will seek to reduce our transportation-related carbon footprint 20-30% by 2020."

These goals are quite timely and appear to be attainable. There are most definitely aspects of the campus such as transportation that can be enhanced in order to benefit the community. The same document also states another important goal in developing a sustainable transportation network:

"A transportation system that prioritizes walking, biking, and public transport for on -campus and short--distance travel, and offers commuters viable alternatives to driving alone."

Among the many goals set by the institution, Miami has organizations and clubs related to sustainability such as the Green Team, the assignment of Eco Reps to dorms, and an annual intercollegiate recycling contest called Recyclemania. There is yet another large ongoing project on campus that will be finished in 2014 which is the construction of the Armstrong Student Center. This building will be abundant with green design features and will undoubtedly display Miami's righteous commitment to sustainability.

Miami Bike Share: There are many practical alternatives to this current dilemma. One action that can be taken by dedicated students is the implementation of solar powered rent-a-bike stations. These stations can be strategically placed all throughout campus, and be used by any student or faculty member. A bike could be accessed with just a swipe of their Miami ID card and charge them $0.25 (or another fair price) for the duration of their ride. Once arriving at the desired location, the student or faculty member can turn in the bicycle at another station nearby. This concept gives all students the ability get some exercise while on their way to class or even just sleep in those extra ten minutes and still be on time to their 8:00 A.M. class. As David Holtzman discusses in his article "Share-A-Bike", knowing how many students would take advantage of such a program, the money that would be spent on these machines could undoubtedly pay for the systems themselves within the first year.

Electric Light Rail System: Another change that can be made relates to the inefficient empty buses that run over ten hours most days of the week, wasting campus money and gasoline that is used to fuel them. A rational substitute for these smog belching machines is a zero emission, light rail system (or sometimes called a "street car"). Places like Zurich, Switzerland and Portland, Oregon already use this method of public transportation and are reported to have relatively less traffic at all times of the day because of it. A relatively new light rail system runs right through the Portland State University campus and provides students with access to their classes along with places like the local farmer's market. Modern light rail systems are flexible and adaptable. They can be set up in a manner that still allows access for cars throughout the campus, but who needs a car when there is a free light rail system that can take you anywhere you need within five minutes? Perhaps this method of transportation would take a few years to plan out and construct, but it would have an enormous environmental and transportation efficiency impact at Miami.

Mobile Sustainable Beverage Shop: The final proposition that can be made is the addition of a mobile beverage shop. In order to fix the problem of the few too many Starbucks shops located across campus; Miami can partner with Starbucks and create a mobile bar that serves Starbucks coffee. To further prove that Miami is Sustainable, the mobile shop can be one-hundred percent environmentally friendly. This means it would be made from recyclable, renewable, and natural materials such as bamboo, hemp, and recycled rubber. The cups, utensils and silverware, (which at most other quick stop food joints would be used once and then thrown away), can all be biodegradable and recycled at nearby bins. The portable kiosk itself can be driven by a bicycle connected to it, while all the appliances stowed in a space saving fashion are powered by a solar panel on the roof of the contraption.

Whenever developing a proposition, it is frequently the case that one's proposal will have its benefits that will come in some form of cost. In this case, some may argue that financial issues may arise and thwart the progress of initiating these three creative solutions. Money is almost always a necessity when trying to bring about change. Seemingly high costs for light rail systems ignore the fact that the current Miami Metro bus system guzzles hundreds of gallons of gas a day along with the deterioration of Miami's wallet.

There are various impacts when instigating transportation upgrades in a community, and in this case; the benefits undeniably outweigh the risks and setbacks. The most important advantages of these solutions are the improved health of students and faculty, reduced energy and fuel costs, and the overall increase in transportation efficiency.

Miami Bike Share (Impact): After bestowing integrated rent-a-bike stations all over campus, student and faculty health would most likely be improved significantly. This would be due not only to the obvious fact that riding a bike to class burns calories, but for every student that decided to bike to class instead of drive, they would avoid *six tons* of carbon dioxide from being emitted into Oxford's air every year. Riding a bike around campus also benefits time management for college students and increases efficiency. Another benefit of these rent-a-bike stations is that they could bring in revenue for the university. This income could go to a variety of causes such as other sustainable alterations on campus or even some other kind of humanitarian charity of the school's choice.

Electric Light Rail System (Impact): Once the electric light rail system is fabricated, traffic all around campus would be reduced. Fewer students will feel the need to drive to class and can keep their cars in parking lots close by while they ride the efficient light rail system that will get them anywhere they need to be in Oxford. Likewise, energy and fuel costs paid by Miami will also be reduced. An energy efficient light rail system would run on electricity; eliminating all gasoline costs and CO_2 emissions. (The chart below is from Patrick Condon's article "Why a Street Car is Something to be Desired"). Not

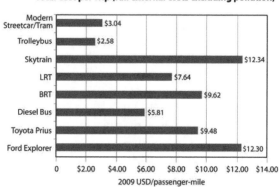

only does it save the university money, but the Center for Neighborhood Technology (CNT) has proven that consumers who take mass transit in place of owning cars spend a far smaller fraction of their total income on transit costs. An additional benefit is that efficient transportation might help attract new students to this beautiful campus.

Mobile Sustainable Beverage Shop (Impact): Subsequently, the addition of a mobile sustainable beverage shop would allow for the widespread campus enjoyment of Starbucks favorites even on those mornings when time is crucial. The environmentally friendly features will encourage green innovation on campus and give a fresh and exciting fulfillment in buying your morning coffee. In Peter Fisk's award-winning book *People, Planet, Profit*, he discusses ways that sustainability drives innovation and growth. In essence of his book, this is also a quality business proposal given that it has the ability of profiting off of benefitting students, faculty and the environment.

Considering that the town of Oxford was established two centuries years ago, it is easy to see that the community has come a long way since then. The environmentally friendly 2014 Armstrong Student Center is eagerly awaited and the numerous other steps the university has already taken to encourage sustainability on campus are truly inspiring. Nonetheless, the proposals discussed above are innovative ideas that some schools like Portland State University are already benefiting from and could have the same impact at Miami. Knowing that these deviations in transportation could improve student and faculty health, reduce traffic, increase energy efficiency, save money, and benefit the environment seem like obvious reasons to start implementing them.

Petition for Bike Sharing at Miami

Miami University is a wonderful place to live. I enjoy taking a stroll around campus and witnessing the colors of fall blend with the colonial brick buildings that make this place feel like home. It is unfortunate, however, when I reach the intersection of Patterson Avenue and Spring Street and am woken from my day dream by the hazy congestion of exhaust belching vehicles. As of now, Miami's primary means of transportation include walking, driving and biking. Most underclassmen don't have cars on campus mostly because the university advises against it and there are limited free parking spaces. This turns a five minute drive from East campus to the recreation center into a thirty minute walk. As a college student, one's time is already limited, and spending twenty to thirty minutes walking *anywhere* is a hindrance that most underclassmen must face at Miami at one point or another. That is why some alternate forms of efficient transportation around Miami's campus are an essential tactic in improving the institution as a whole.

There are many practical alternatives to this current dilemma. One action that can be taken by parking and transportation services is the implementation of solar powered rent-a-bike stations. These stations can be strategically placed all throughout campus, and be used by any student or faculty member. A bike could be accessed with just a swipe of their Miami ID card and access a charge of $0.25 for the duration of their ride. Once arriving at the desired location, the student or faculty member can turn in the bicycle at another station nearby. This concept gives all students the ability get some exercise while on their way to class or even just sleep in those extra ten minutes and still be on time to their 8:00 A.M. class.

By investing in integrated rent-a-bike stations all over campus, student and faculty health would be improved significantly. This would be due not only to the obvious fact that riding a bike to class burns calories, but for every student that decided to bike to class instead of drive, they would avoid *six tons* of carbon dioxide from being emitted into Oxford's air every year. Riding a bike around campus also benefits time management for college students and increases efficiency. Another benefit of these rent-a-bike stations is that they could bring in revenue for the university. This income could go to a variety of causes such as other sustainable alterations on campus or even some other kind of humanitarian charity of the school's choice. Either way, this would be a huge step in sustainability at Miami. In the "Miami University Sustainability Commitments and Goals" of 2011, it proudly stated that:

> "Because sustainability comes not only through what we do, but how we invest our money, Miami University and the Miami University Foundation will work to bring more transparency and social responsibility to investment decisions."

There cannot possibly be a better investment than preserving the habitat on which this treasure of an institution was founded upon. We, as students and faculty need to take care of our school and our environment to guarantee that this prestigious university exists "forever and a day.

Works Cited

Condon, Patrick. "Why a Streetcar Is Something to Be Desired." *The Tyee*. 2010. Web. 23 Oct. 2012.

Fisk, Peter. *People, Planet, Profit: How to Embrace Sustainability for Inno vation and Business Growth*. London: Kogan Page, 2010. Print. 20 Oct. 2012

"Future Armstrong Student Center." *Environmental Sustainability*. Mi ami University, 2011. Web. 22 Oct. 2012.

Holtzman, David. "Share-A-Bike." *Transportation Research Board* (2008): Web. 21 Oct. 2012.

Miami University Sustainability Commitments and Goals of 2011: <http://www.miamialum.org/s/916/images/editor_docum ents/Email/PresidentsOffice/May2011-SustainabilityCom mitmentsGoals.pdf>

Posner, Andrew. "Bike Share Programs Becoming Increasingly Popu lar on College Campuses." *TreeHugger*. 2008. Web. 22 Oct. 2012.

Editorial Team's Note

Hunter Leachman's proposal on transportation efficiency offers detailed analysis of a localized public issue grounded in a thoughtful yet critical analysis of official Miami University documentation. When making a public argument, it is not always easy to see or fully discuss the local impact of larger political debates. In calling for campus innovations and reforms, however, Leachman begins with a thorough recognition of already existing efforts to make Miami's campus more eco-friendly, a move that strengthens his credibility as a writer. Consider Leachman's personal narrative in his essay, which provides "thick" or detailed description of real issues impacting his day-to-day work at Miami. Leachman, in short, does an exemplary job of expressing his personal interest in this topic and the ways local and national contexts inform and continue to shape one another. As a Miami student, what local issues concern you? Also, consider audience. How would Leachman need to shift his rhetoric if he were addressing a primarily student-based audience — in what ways might his proposal look different?

Inquiry Four: Remediation

Cyber Bullying Must Stop
Jessica Garrison

This project can be found on the *CCM* **Online.**

Writer's Reflection

When I was assigned this project, I immediately knew I wanted my topic to be on cyber bullying. I wanted to educate my audience on the increasing percentages of teens who have been victim to this form of bullying and I also wanted to give statistics and warning signs of teens that are cyber bullies themselves. This is a very real issue in today's technological world and shouldn't be taken so lightly. I chose to use iMovie, which allowed me to incorporate several tools to create an effective short film.

By using iMovie, I included music, picture, text and video that all tied together to get my argument across that cyber bullying is an issue that people need to be aware of. A friend and I made fake Facebook profiles with exaggerated names such as Chloe CyberBully Smith and Nicole CriesAlot Jones. This allowed me to take screenshots and videos of the dramatized cyber bullying that I added into my project. All of the things that the "Chloe" wrote to "Nicole" were versions of examples I came across on the Internet. The way I set up my project was I had a statistic the audience could read, and then change to a screen video of an example of cyber bullying that related to the fact.

The audience I was aiming for was mainly parents, although any age group would be benefit from it. Parents were my main focus because they hold the most power when it comes to their children and the way they understand the Internet. Some adults with children who have online profiles admit they generally don't know how to use it, therefore they don't know how their children are using it. By reading facts and actually being able to see a visual of how Facebook can be used, it gives them a better understanding of what goes on. When I first began the project, I absentmindedly assumed my audience would understand Facebook lingo and how it works. I had to better show and explain what a "wall post" or a "status" was.

I'm most proud of the iMovie I made because that is a program I love working with and spent a lot of time on. I liked how this project went beyond the traditional style of writing and allowed me to get my point across through other methods. I believe I came up with a unique way to portray the issue of cyber bullying, which directly tied to the issue itself.

Some of the benefits I had from inquiry 3 was most of the statistics I had included in my paper, I used in my movie. My paper was filled with secondary sources and information regarded kids and social media, so I could just skim my paper and find an example to use. One limit to having a movie instead of something like a Prezi or a PowerPoint is it's more difficult to have a lot of text information. I tried to keep my information short so the movie wouldn't just be reading facts. However, a benefit is that the audience can clearly see the example being illustrated which helps to support the awareness of the issue.

Editorial Team's Note
View Jessica Garrison's video **on the *CCM* website**. In this video, Garrison takes a compelling stance against cyber bullying by using the affordances of screencasting technology. Garrison's forethought to create mock Facebook profiles to perform her argument demonstrates the careful rhetorical work that goes into composing effective multimodal projects. Not only does she use screencasting to her benefit but she also makes savvy music and transition choices throughout her argument. Garrison's work also demonstrates the rhetorical potential for assemblage, as she crafts her argument by incorporating persuasive already-existing footage on YouTube. By doing this, Garrison invites her viewers to consider a particularly troubling cyber bullying case. In terms of editing video, notice how Garrison sustains consistency throughout her project. What are some ways to keep multimodal projects stylistically consistent?

Childhood Cancer: Little Patients, Little Patience
Jake Prodoehl

This project can be found on the *CCM* **Online.**

Writer's Reflection

I loved the Inquiry Four assignment! I am obviously very passionate about my topic of childhood cancer and to be able to put my argument into pictures and videos (what I focus on in my work with the I Back Jack Foundation), I knew I would really enjoy this Inquiry. As I found my Tumblr posts, I knew exactly which ones would work and which ones would not. However, once I sat down to start writing the essay portion of Inquiry Four, I found myself struggling. I find it hard to put into words the actions you take to convince and argument. Yes, some points came easier than others but as a whole, I had more trouble on this section than I thought I would.

I have three paragraphs that I consider to be my best. First, I love my original post of the pictures of Jack and I and also the quote at the bottom. I actually have never seen that quote until I was looking for posts for my Tumblr blog. The quote spoke to me because I could completely relate to it. Second, I love when I talked about my thought process with my last post. One day is all it takes - and everyone has been in a situation that has proved that to be true, for better or for worse. The balloon and the quote combined to make the absolute perfect closing post, in my opinion. Finally, I loved explaining my reasoning behind my title change. The new title actually came to me over Thanksgiving break when a family member told me that Jack must have had so much patience. Then it hit me! Overall, this was a great assignment!

◆ ◆ ◆

For my Inquiry Four assignment, I have made it my mission and goal to raise awareness of childhood cancer while recruiting young adults to join the movement and make a difference in the lives of children fighting cancer. These little patients are losing patience as no progress is being made. The visual aspects, in particular, of Tumblr will help me in my goal and hopefully cure these little patients of the horrible monster called cancer.

To start my Tumblr blog, I knew exactly what my first and most visible post would be. I made a picture collage of my personal relationship with Jack Bartosz, my hero, who lost his battle with Neuroblastoma in August of this year. I hope that these pictures and the quote at the bottom will be able to make childhood cancer more personable for my audience. Realistically speaking, my audience most likely does not know a child fighting cancer. But if I include pictures of my relationship to childhood cancer, it is my hope that my audience will be more able to relate and therefore feel the need to make a difference. The first picture is a photo of Jack and I on Jack's tenth birthday. Below that, there are pictures of the I Back Jack Foundation's logo, a note I received from Jack, Jack next to the Wheaties box that he appeared on with Superbowl MVP, Aaron Rodgers, and finally, a picture that I took of Jack in the hospital after receiving chemotherapy. These make pediatric cancer seem more "real" as opposed to reading an occasional newspaper article.

Following my most visible post, I have more pictures and visual representations of statistics. I am a firm believer that nothing is more powerful than two things: pictures and music. That is the glory of social media – the ability to portray emotions not through monotone words, but through emotional and though provoking pictures and music. On my blog, my audience can find my favorite video produced by the I Back Jack Foundation and myself. The video is of Jack in a Milwaukee newsroom, educating his own audience about childhood cancer and what people can do to make a difference. After watching this video again recently, I realized that Jack's audience would become my audience for my Tumblr blog: young adults who have the potential to make a difference. Using Tumblr, I can easily utilize both original pictures and music as well as incorporating those aspects from other blogs. In Tumblr, text can be very effective. However, Tumblr users tend to quickly skim through blogs until they find an interesting picture or sound clip. People are naturally drawn to visual and audio representations as opposed to long texts. I took full advantage of this and composed my blog of mostly pictures, videos, and music.

I closed my Tumblr blog with a powerful picture of a balloon floating into the sky with a quote asking the audience to at least think about childhood cancer for just today. In my eyes this was the perfect closing post because in reality, that is all it takes: one day. As everyone knows, one day, one afternoon, one moment, can change the rest of your life. If I can convince my audience to not only look at pictures and listen to stories about childhood cancer victims, but to actually take a moment away from the computer screen to think about childhood cancer, then I succeeded in my mission. I can really relate to thinking about childhood cancer despite not knowing a thing about it before I got involved with Jack. A while ago, a friend asked me to help pass out flyers for some organization called the "I Back Jack Foundation." So I decided to help and after passing out the "Beat childhood cancer" flyers, I was driving home without the music on just thinking. This snowballed into planning World Record setting events with the foundation and meeting my hero. It changed my life forever. I not only want, but I need my audience to think about childhood cancer and think about how they can truly make a difference!

In regards to the format of my blog, I believe that the format I selected best appeals to my audience of young adults, as it is clear, easy to follow, and organized. If my audience is honestly interested in making a difference and donating their time and efforts, they do not want all of the "glitz and glamour" of Tumblr. They want to be emotionally attached to the cause. They want to be informed about the severity of the issue and the importance of now. They want to make a difference. None of these include fancy fonts or sparkles. All that is required is pure emotion and I believe that is portrayed through my use of visuals: pictures of Jack, visual representations of statistics, pictures of Ronan (who Taylor Swift's new single, "Ronan," is based off of), and videos from childhood cancer awareness groups.

As I reviewed my final Tumblr blog, there was one thing I realized I needed to change. Originally, my title was "Inquiry Four: Fighting Childhood Cancer." This title was good but came across too much like an assignment instead of a mission. So I dropped the "Inquiry Four" from the title, but I still wasn't completely satisfied. What could I do that would really hook my audience from the start? What would make them starting thinking about childhood cancer right away? And then it came to me... "Childhood Cancer: Little Patients, Little Patience." I made my topic clear when I stated childhood cancer. But, the subtitle would really make my audience take into consideration timeliness and why getting involved right now is so important. Little Patients, Little Patience. Now is the time to make a difference because there is no time like the present!

In conclusion, I think the format and organization of my Tumblr blog perfectly adhere to the expectations and needs of potential volunteers in the fight against pediatric cancer. My two main goals were to make cancer relatable and to get my audience to think about cancer away from the computer screen. I believe I accomplished these goals with my original posts showing pictures of Jack and myself. Additionally I think my last post left the perfect image in my audience's head. Together, we can all make a difference! Let's give these little patients a little more patience in their heroic fight against cancer.

Editorial Team's Note
View Jake Prodoehl's tumblr, **featured on the *CCM* website**, and consider his reflective analysis. Prodoehl's goals in this project are to reach audiences in digital spaces in order to both raise awareness of

childhood cancer and encourage young adults to support curing cancer. While the topic of childhood cancer is large and complex, what Prodoehl does well is that he narrows his scope from the very beginning of the project. He starts with his friendship with Jack Bartosz, a victim of childhood cancer, along with his passion for and investment in the non-profit organization, I Back Jack. Because he narrows his focus to a specific audience and purpose, Prodoehl is able to cater his tumblr site to his goals through everything from the title of his site, the images he uses, to the organization of the site. The specific choices Prodoehl makes, which he documents in his reflective analysis, are made in an effort to, as he writes, "make pediatric cancer seem more 'real' as opposed to reading an occasional newspaper article." As noted in his reflective analysis, Prodoehl made several changes to key parts of his Tumblr site before arriving at his final draft. How is revising a digital composition different from revising an essay? How is Tumblr different from other digital spaces, such as Youtube or Facebook? How were his choices influenced by his specific audience, purpose, as well as his medium?

Inquiry Five: Final Reflection

English 111 Portfolio: What It's All About

Ashley Hopes

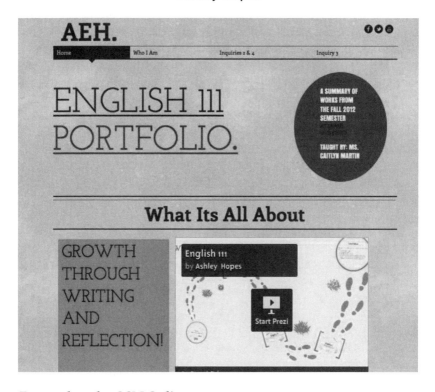

Featured on the *CCM Online*

Editorial Team's Note

In this online portfolio, Ashley Hopes reflects on her experiences in ENG 111 through an unusual medium: Prezi. This Prezi connects specific outcomes for each Inquiry to her own experiences as a writer and rhetor, allowing us to see where she excelled--as well as where she stumbled. This kind of honest detail is key to meaningful reflection. How does the medium of her reflection (Prezi) change the claims she makes about herself? What does this medium allow her to do (and how does it restrict what she can say)? Also consider how the arrangement of her online portfolio encourages readers to engage with her writing in very specific ways. How does her arrangement impact how we read and understand her work in ENG 111?

We have several great multi-modal reflections that could not be printed. Please visit the *CCM's* **companion website** to see all the different ways reflection can be done (other than a print essay).

The Mirror of English 111: A Reflection
Maisie Laud

The word "essay" is defined as "a short literary composition dealing with a subject." It comes from the Latin, exigere, meaning to investigate. It makes sense that an essay is an investigation. A writer must dive deep into whatever subject they are writing about to present a logical opinion or position, the thesis. That position is to be supported with evidence, the body. And, finally, concluded. As simple as it sounds to write an essay, it requires a lot of brainpower. English 111 has taught me that writing an essay is more than just words on a paper; it is about a powerful, passionate discussion issued as persuasion that just so happens to take place on a document.

The first time I wrote an essay that was meaningful enough for me to remember was a reflection I wrote as a sophomore in high school. The reflection was based upon a traumatic experience I suffered in 8th grade. I remember taking my essay to my teacher to proof read and give me some constructive criticism. His one expression was, "wow." He told me that my writing sent shivers down his back and that he could feel every description I wrote as if he were right there with me. That simple comment changed my world. I finally thought of myself as a writer. I can think back to 3rd grade when the concept of an essay was introduced to my class of timid eight year olds. We had no idea how to argue anything, especially any proposed essay topic. The next thing that pops into my head regarding writing was a research paper I had to do in the 5th grade about the mummification process in ancient Egypt. For that, we were allotted five months. It seems so long compared to the two weeks I've been allotted for most of the inquiries this semester. The next most significant experience was a class I took as a junior in creative writing. I found a true passion in writing from this class. Creative writing was a blank "canvas" in which I had barely drawn on, but this class let me use any medium I could get my hands on to express any type of fiction writing. I wrote a five thousand-word short story on shampoo that was widely lauded by my peers and my teacher. I like to constitute writers as anyone who likes to write and would do it in their free time alongside any compulsory writing, and for that, I label myself as a writer.

My writing process throughout my life has evolved. I used to look upon compulsory rough drafts as a bore, and did not give them my full effort. It was not until I was pushed into the deep end of writing in high school that I managed to see these mandatory drafts (which were no longer mandatory) as predominantly helpful. Now, I try to always create an outline before I start writing. As a college writer, I have grown more comfortable with my essay-writing process. It begins with a rough idea, which will ultimately become the introduction paragraph and a slightly more developed version of this 'idea' becomes my thesis. This idea requires support, and thusly creates a rough outline for the body of the essay. The conclusion sums up the points I have designed as support for the thesis, restates the thesis in a different manner, and possibly introduces a thought to leave the reader with, to contemplate further. I like to keep a template like this to reflect upon. If I am lost in the process, I try hard to organize every one of my thoughts about my paper into one of the support paragraphs. After creating this outline, I give myself a day or so to let any further ideas gel or skim through the material about which I am writing. Once my outline is created, and my ideas have gelled, I 'hop to it.' I immediately sit down and write for at least one hour. Then I usually get sleepy and fall asleep. Ill wake up the next morning having dreamt about something completely irrelevant, but have a blast of creativity that could add a lot to my essay. I have to jot down all those notes before I forget them. Then, when I'm in the shower, I'll think of another valuable point, that which I scribble down on another post-it note. That night I will begin writing again, incorporating all these extra thoughts into my writing, just to begin the process over again. I can't write with hip-hop music on or else I will incorporate the lyrics into my writing subconsciously. If I choose to write with music playing, it must be John Coltrane or Miles Davis. I do not want to characterize my writing too much, because the entire process is subject to change, and is constantly evolving to better suit my needs as a writer.

Several of my strengths have been highlighted throughout English III both in the classroom, and on writing. One of my strengths that I am vehemently aware of is my ability to defend. I do not shy away from arguments when they are presented, that is, if I am informed about the subject. I have noticed this in class when we are presenting our articles. Miami University has many, many fervent

Republican students. I, on the other hand, am quite the Liberal. This makes it pretty easy for me to fall into arguments. Since journalists are meant to provide a neutral diagnosis of whatever they are covering, I find it easy for the presenter of the article to give their opinion...and wherever there is an opinion, there is a counter opinion, and I usually jump to that. Another way to look at this is my ability to defend an argument through writing. Inquiry 3 required students to pick a side of a public argument and support a thesis of why we chose whichever side. In my inquiry 3, I defended the statement that television should be more closely monitored to try and eliminate any racial content. I researched a lot for this argument because it is definitely a topic that I encounter daily: watching television. The opening of my essay talks about the dark hole of racism that America has been trying desperately to climb out of for a long, long time, only to be pushed further down into by outside catalysts, such as the media. What I think it most powerful about this essay, which helps defend my argument, is that I brought in this metaphor of the 'dark hole' to symbolize a change that needs to be made, more, as my thesis states, closely monitored. I make the opening of my argument very broad and general, so that readers have something in common with the opening, which further drags them into reading.

Another strength I have is my ability to relay anecdotes. This might also be considered a weakness, and I will get to that. In every writer's memo I've written concerning a reflection, I specify how easy it is for me to write about myself. Someone once told me to "write what I know." Inquiry 1 required students to reflect upon themselves. "Phew," I thought. "If this is the kind of writing I will be doing for my first semester of English, then bring it on," I jested. Inquiry 1 came and went with ease, for it was primarily a reflection upon my previous writing, something that came easily to me. The other assignment that had me eager to do well on was Inquiry 4, a media representation. After seeing the examples presented in class, I had a spark of genius. Shakespeare: my one true literary and theatrical love. I've studied Shakespeare since the seventh grade, and have loved nearly all of it. I've acted in Shakespeare plays, I have dissected them in class, and I have read them in my free time. "Why not do something about Shakespeare?" I thought. It is not generally easy, but those words flow naturally with me, and I am passionate about it. It seemed like the perfect project, and so began my "42 Phrases Coined by Shakespeare that We Use Today." The one thing I know best is myself and I think I have a very clear, deliberate, and fun sense in writing about myself.

Connecting onto the way I write anecdotes is the way I write about something when I am passionate about it. This includes my Inquiry 4 concerning William Shakespeare, but I am aiming to focus this more on my Inquiry 2: the rhetorical analysis. I searched high and low for a speech to dissect that was not cliché or one that someone else had already chosen. Having a background in theater makes it super easy for me to look to a binder of monologues I've acquired throughout my theatrical pursuits, so I took a gander through those selections. The one that stuck out to me, the one that clearly highlighted logos, the logical standpoint of a speech, pathos, the emotional connection of the speaker to the audience, and ethos, the clarity of the speech, was a soliloquy from The Laramie Project, a non-fictional play. The speech comes from the father of a murdered son to a courtroom, as a statement. I went to a high school that was all about acceptance. When I first read this play, it really hit home for me, because it was so upsettingly real. I think that is what made my rhetorical analysis so powerful, was that I was so strongly connected to the play, its meaning, and the speech itself.

I am fairly confident in my writing except for one thing. My primary weakness is the research paper. Whenever I dote upon being able to write about myself, I am disgusted about how narcissistic it sounds. I love to write about myself. Unfortunately, this does point to my downfall when it comes to writing. I think I have spent too much time writing fiction and creative writing that I have lacked a better education in the argument department. I did say before that I am able to defend well. I still believe this to be true, but for some reason, my research papers always come to defy that. I really enjoyed how easy my teacher made it for my English III class to accomplish Inquiry 3, however, I still feel that that is where my true weakness falls.

I have said time and again that one day I will write for Saturday Night Live, the infamous comedy sketch show on NBC. I realize that English III does not focus on script writings or satire. I also realize that my goals as a comedy writer are terribly outlandish and farfetched. I do plan on taking every advantage of my writing classes in college to help in my pursuit of comedy writing. The things I've learned in my time in high school and in the first semester of college are very concrete in regards to writings. They are aspects and tools about analysis, arguments, and general reflection that I will carry with me far into any career I choose. My father has told me many times about how, "people these days can't write." He works with people who submit reports and portfolios and finds himself chuckling over how many grammatical or syntax errors there are in their writing. I hope the skill set I have been blessed with throughout my academic life will prevent my future bosses from reading ill-proof read reports of mine, for I will be able to submit them with confidence.

English 111 has been successful in cluing me into the tools I need to take with me as I dive further into the pool of college writing, and onward into the field of writing in whatever I choose to do with my life. I see a defined change in my writing between Inquiry 1 and Inquiry 2. Inquiry 1 was very personable. It was a little abstract, but for the most part, easy to understand. The writing was a little aloof. The writing in my Inquiry 2 was definitely more concrete. The concepts were straight and to the point, for the sake of my analysis. I notice that a lot of my writing from high school carries the same quality as inquiry 1, an aloof, abstract way of writing and analyzing. Inquiry 2 represents the more logical, more well thought out piece of writing. The most important tool I have developed and will carry with me throughout my writing career is that of creating an outline. Creating an outline helps me organize my thesis with my respective supportive points. I pledge to not take for granted my ability to sit down and start writings, because this has proven to be one of my less attractive habits, and I end up with an unorganized cloud of words rather than an organized, well thought out essay. Being able to present and defend a clear point will help me with my next important tool. I have developed a sense of confidence with my writing that shines through when I know I have created something great. I also pledge, in addition to creating an outline and being a confident writer, to take every advantage of any aid I can get for my writing. It has been such a privilege to work with caring teachers and tutors who want to see me succeed. I take all points and criticisms and remember them to make sure I don't make the same mistakes on my next paper. I vow to be smart about my outline logic, and only present essays once they have been organized and written to my best ability, as well as sifted through with a fine tooth comb for any errors. All these tools, which have proved to help with my personal success, will help me prove excellence with future writing endeavors.

What I left out in my definition of "essay" was that it also comes from a variation on the Latin word "agere" meaning to compel. Essays are meant to persuade and do so by compiling support and verification towards an argument. English 111 breaks down the various aspects needed in a persuasive, compelling essay into five inquiries, all specified and devoted to different means of persuasion. By breaking down the means of compiling a compelling essay, English 111 helps to develop a polished set of skills, each finely tuned for subsequent use.

Editorial Team's Note
The strength of Maisie Laud's reflective essay is her willingness to assess her own work. It is not easy to take a critical eye toward your own writing, but Laud does. She begins this essay by explaining what an essay can do--it is a way to investigate. She then works through an analysis of her writing and herself as a writer. She does this with compelling voice and style, and narrates the exploration in a manner that is entertaining and engaging. Most importantly, Laud evaluates her strengths and her weaknesses, and provides substantial evidence. All of this supports her larger claim--that writing is a way to persuade by building evidence toward an argument. Finally, Laud concludes with the meaning of essay as "to compel"--reminding us of the whole point of building a persuasive essay with carefully chosen evidence — to compel an audience to listen to what the writer has to say.

English 112 Essays

Course Description

ENG 112

English 112, Composition and Literature, is designed to get you thinking critically about texts. "Texts" in this case could be anything from Charles Dickens' *A Tale of Two Cities* to a Katy Perry music video (as you'll see in one of the writing samples for Inquiry 1). In this class, you will hone the skills needed to be able to read, annotate, analyze, and write about texts at a collegiate-level. As you make your way through the chosen class texts, you will learn various tools for how to analyze and critically read those texts, and will in turn create your own texts –a critical response to what you have read. This class will help expand your understanding of what, exactly, constitutes a text through examining literature, secondary sources, movies, blog posts, and even social media. Examining these different texts will help you learn and strengthen your techniques for responding to, interpreting, critiquing, and evaluating texts, which will in turn help you write research-based arguments about texts for academic, disciplinary audiences.

ENG 112 is centered around four major writing inquiries, samples of which are included in this section:

Inquiry 1: Close, Critical Reading
In this inquiry, you will closely examine and critically engage with texts. Some examples of this type of engagement include Maisie Laud's "Soft Rain on a Hot Mind" and Jarred Gerry's "Feminist Dream," which examine Ray Bradbury's *There Will Come Soft Rains* and Katy Perry's "Wide Awake" music video, respectively. Both these essays engage questions such as: "What is this text about?" "What strategies does this text use to create meaning?" "What effects does this text have?" Critical reading essays generally analyze short texts, such as a section of a speech, a dialogue in a play or novel, or the visual elements of a website. Laud does this specifically through examining a single sentence out of Bradbury's entire text.

Inquiry 2: Cultural / Historical Analysis (Parts A & B)

The second inquiry of ENG112 is normally divided into two parts, A and B. Part A centers on researching the culture and/or history of a text, while in Part B you'll use that research to make an informed argument about a text. All texts are distributed and circulated in particular contexts that change over time—and those changes affect texts' meanings. For instance, Shakespeare's *Othello* was originally written and seen by audiences in Elizabethan England, a strikingly different historical context than that of modern day. In this section, you'll find two examples of Part B essays: Beasy Jennison's "America The Beautiful?" and Brian Jong's "Class Divide in the Hunger Games and American Society". Jennison demonstrates how the anxious culture of Post-World War II America influenced the reception of Robert Franks *The Americans*. Jong, on the other hand, looks at modern day America, but examines what a contemporary novel, *The Hunger Games*, reveals about the current social class system.

Inquiry 3: Creative and Critical Engagement

In Inquiry Three, you will focus on applying the close reading and cultural investigation skills you've developed in your first two Inquiries to rework, challenge, or respond to existing arguments and texts surrounding a public issue for non-academic contexts and audiences. There are two parts to this Inquiry. First, you will locate and analyze a set of primary public texts, and then you'll produce a text (other than an academic essay) that dialogues with these primary works in some way for a public venue. For instance, you may be asked to create an iMovie or WeVideo project, like Tio Davis's Youtube video series on teen suicide, or you might re-work a public argument or literary text in a new genre. Jia Yao Wang, for example, changes casual conversations between international English 112 students into a short fiction in order to communicate the unique challenges faced by English learners here at Miami. Both of these projects, essentially, use non-academic modes of composition in order to comment on and respond to public issues they each consider important.

Inquiry 4: Final/Comprehensive Reflection

The fourth and final inquiry builds from critical reflection of your own reading and writing that you will engage in throughout the course.

Just as you have done for every major assignment, you will be asked to think critically and carefully about your reading processes and rhetorical composing choices. Inquiry 4 asks you to do this through an extended essay about your learning in the course and how you have met the specific course outcomes — but your focus in this essay should be broader than merely the ENG 112 course. You might be invited to examine and reflect on your recent experiences as a writer and communicator, or your entire writing history and possible future. Tina Kinstedt and Tio Davis use the genre of letter writing to think through their experiences in their first year as a college writer and imagine the past and future selves who benefit from the lessons learned. Both writers were asked to collect and submit a portfolio of their body of work for English 112. You may be asked to complete a similar portfolio and may consider the benefits of using traditional word documents like Kinstedt and Andrew Frondorf, or digital web-building software like Davis.

Inquiry One: Close, Critical Reading

Feminist Dream

Jarred Gerry

Writer's Reflection

Ever since first hearing Katy Perry on the radio singing her first single "I Kissed a Girl," I knew she was going to be a star. Her *Teenage Dream* album was the summer playlist for radio stations and teenagers around the world, and as the years passed by, Katy Perry did indeed become a star… And I became obsessed. I went, and still go through stages where the only song that is played on my iPod, or in my room is one sang by Katy Perry. No song by Perry is safe from the wrath of my voice; but hey, at least I think I do her some justice. So, when first reading the Inquiry One prompt, I immediately knew that the text I would focus my paper on was going to be the "Wide Awake" music video. The first time I saw the video I was completely captivated by the different elements that were presented throughout, but it wasn't until I began to critically "read" the video until I became aware of how influential the music video really is when it comes to gendering.

Close and critical reading was quite an enjoyable task to be completely honest. Of the 127,553, 455 views that the "Wide Awake" music video has received, I alone probably contributed a good 105 views. I watched the music video over and over and over and over again, taking notes on the setting, the characters, and the characters actions, as well as teaching my roommate a thing or two on how to truly belt out the best rendition of "Wide Awake." The notes I took helped me to connect my ideas and allowed me to identify topoi and other significant information that I thought should have been analyzed. I wanted to avoid looking at lyrics themselves because I don't think they held as much substance as the video.

At first, I was quite hesitant of whether or not this text choice was appropriate, and I was worried if the video even held enough substance, but after emailing my professor, I was glad to hear that she thought the text I chose was a great choice. After banging my head against the wall in frustration of not knowing what exactly to do with my notes, and listening to my Katy Perry playlist, hoping to discover some newfound inspiration, I channeled my inner Perry and devised a plan. I was able to identify three separate stages of the video, which helped me to focus on the way that gender is being done in each segment. I wanted to focus on the way that Perry both obviously and subtly redefines the gender roles that we use today. To do this, I highlighted areas in my notes where I myself found something surprising about the gendering portrayed and how it compares or contrasts to the gender roles that I have been exposed to over the years. For example, I found the scene where Perry punches her Prince Charming extremely surprising, as well as the setting of the video itself. This was quite interesting and I actually learned a lot about how I myself view gender.

The best way that an audience member would achieve a deeper understanding of my essay and the primary text would be to view the "Wide Awake" music video themselves. I would suggest watching the video for a first time as a regular audience member, only focusing on the video itself. Then, after reading my essay, I suggest watching the video another time around and see whether or not they take the same things away, or if they discover something new. This will help to connect ideas and the audience will have a chance to make their own, personal, connections.

All in all, I had a great time with this inquiry. I not only enjoyed the prompt, but I learned a lot about myself and how I perceive gender in my everyday life.

◆ ◆ ◆

Since 1987, Michael Jackson has been the only artist to have five different songs from one album become a number one single on Billboard's Hot 100 Chart. That is, until a new face emerged and made a momentous splash in not only the music industry, but in households across the world. Katy Perry has been the only artist to tie Michael Jackson's record with five number one singles, which were all from her debut album Teenage Dream, released in 2010. From her more inspirational songs such as "Firework," to her upbeat and peppy "Part of Me," Katy Perry has instilled confidence and individuality in her young, often teenage, female fans through her powerful lyrics and moving videos. In her most recent single "Wide Awake," Katy Perry sings of a troubled girl who is lost in a world where the disquieting reality she faces is far from the fantasy she so desired. Although the lyrics themselves carry a significant amount of meaning, the music video for "Wide Awake" presents an analytical gold mine of insights into the seemingly shunned world of feminism that Perry presents and then tears apart segment by segment. In the "Wide Awake" music video, Katy Perry redefines the 'traditional' gender roles of society and shines a much sought-after light on a new wave of feminism and individuality through the video's presentation of setting, characters, and the actions of the characters.

Enter Katy Perry, wearing a dark almost black, dress that flows as she stands before her labyrinth. This maze-like complex that awaits her is not only dark, but also rather scary and forbidding. The walls are dark, tall, and covered in a sinister looking vine that snakes its way up and down the labyrinth walls. As Perry continues to lose herself in this labyrinth, the walls that surround her begin to close in, as if they are about to consume her, but the audience witnesses Perry summon her inner strength and determination and she stops the walls from swallowing her whole. Since the first few seconds of the video, Katy Perry has taken all that we assume about her gender and thrown it in the trash. Most media will often stereotype women into a role that is dramatically opposite from the one that Perry takes on, because that is how the audience expects to perceive them. Rarely is an audience exposed to a female figure that dresses in dark clothing and is lost in a world of fear, filth, and frustrations. Too often, females are cast in this mold where bright, or soft cute colors overpower the dark, and plans go perfectly without fault; the female characters are shown as vulnerable, weak, and emotional, but not in this video. Perry has proved that stereotype wrong by stopping the walls that surround her from closing in.

The "Wide Awake" video embraces the topoi of paradox, and appearance versus reality to further break apart the stereotypes of women. An atypical situation appears when Perry calls upon a hero to help her. She sends out a flare of distress that illuminates the sky, and we meet a little girl, no older than ten years of age, who comes running to save Perry. This scenario is atypical in that it was not a man who came to save her, like we so often see in movies. Looking at every superhero movie ever made, one can see that the male superheroes dominate the four or five heroines that already play a minimal role. The paradox occurs with the fact that Perry calls upon a little girl, which is not only surprising, but the qualities of this child seem to be self-contradicting of a hero; she appears small, fragile, and gentle. These are not the qualities we see in the heroes that emerge in blockbuster movies or other music videos, which is where the paradox lies. Nothing about the child screams hero, but this little girl represents so much more than just, well, a little girl, and it is vital that audience members understand that, because these tiny, seemingly insignificant instances are truly grand metaphors for the true determination and moxie of a female.

After the summoning of her hero, Perry comes face to face with a group of paparazzi who, metaphorically and literally, shatter the image of Perry from behind the glass of a mirror. Perry has been scrutinized for her work ever since she was a teenager and released her first album as a gospel singer. Since then, Perry's musical genre has dramatically changed and she herself has gone through hardships, such as her marriage and divorce to comedian Russell Brand, that were plastered throughout the media world. This type of scrutiny must have proved extremely damaging to Perry, but, as we have previously seen, she overcomes and continues on deeper into the labyrinth.

Next, the appearance versus reality topoi comes into play as the little girl is shown pushing a seemingly disoriented Perry through a hospital where two men emerge as to deny their passageway through the halls. Once again, the audience witnesses the true power of a female character when the tiny girl scornfully eyes up the men with blatant authority and crashes her foot on the ground, propelling a shockwave down the hall which sends the two men flying and revitalizes Perry back to consciousness. This display of power is very similar to when Perry stopped the walls from closing in on her, and it reinforces the importance of confidence and power in the female perspective. So, this child who appeared to have the self-contradicting qualities of a hero, really held a large amount of power and bravery, hence the topoi of appearance versus reality. Rarely do we see a female character that harnesses authority and supremacy over other characters, let alone a little girl over two strong men.

The second to last scene of the music video brings the audience to the end of Perry's journey. After escaping the hospital, Perry and her petite sidekick enter a garden filled with beautiful flowers, shrubbery, and even a waterfall. Perry is now wearing a tan dress with pale pink roses strewn about and faux butterflies clipped to her flowing purple hair. Immediately, the audience sees this as completely ordinary, because here are two females in an environment that is "normal" for females, as if this is the only habitat they belong in. The flowers, butterflies, and bright colors are all included in that mold that was referenced before, and it almost confuses the audience. Now, enter Prince Charming. At this point it seems that everything Perry has been working for has come down to this, the stereotypical, and might I add dry and hackneyed, ending that we see in all fairy tales. This gorgeous man dismounts his horse, smiling ear to ear, and walks right up to Perry, where he crosses his fingers behind his back and goes in for everlasting kiss of victory. Katy Perry, who is smarter then she looks, winds up for the right hook to the jaw that sends Prince Charming flying. Perry could not have made a clearer statement; women don't need to rely on men to have the happily ever after ending, especially when the love they are seeking is all a false hope. Through her actions, Perry has made a statement that will be sure to have a lasting effect on any of her audience members, especially those who are younger and grew up on the fairytale belief that without a Prince Charming there is no happy ending.

Katy Perry's video wraps up when she sends her sidekick back home. After a long, well deserved embrace the audience sees the little girl walking away alongside her bicycle, with a pink license place reading "KATHERYN." The little girl who helped Perry through her quest was a younger version of herself, and this reminds the audience that maybe the innocent child we once were could save us from our own misfortunes and challenges by harnessing their true being. The child version of Perry would not have been exposed to the many gendering norms that are present today, so she was over to overcome what the grown up Perry may not have been able to do by herself.

Throughout her video, Katy Perry has redefined the gender roles of both men and women through both her obvious, and sometimes unapparent and deeply rooted sense of individuality and sheer power. Through the three tiered segments composed of unconventional setting, diverse and complex characters, and their stereotype breaking actions, Katy Perry has created a music video that not only redefines gender roles, but offers a refreshing view of feminism that so many of her fans have been waiting for.

Editorial Team's Note
Through a close critical reading of Katy Perry's music video "Wide Awake," Jarred Gerry complicates the ways in which contemporary society, specifically teenage girls, see themselves and understand gender. Flipping the typical fairy tale on its head, Gerry argues that Perry's video redefines stereotypical gender roles by depicting a strong, female character that is capable of overcoming obstacles without the help of a Prince Charming. By examining this music video, Gerry is not only able to tie texts to social issues like gender and feminism, but also shows that close reading isn't limited to literary texts. In addition to looking at an unconventional text through a literary lens, Gerry's essay is also a good example of how critical close reading and literary analysis overlaps with and utilizes similar analytical tools as rhetorical analysis. Gerry's essay offers thick description of Perry's video, as well as uniting rhetorical terms like "topoi" and "audience" to terms more prevalent in literary analysis like "paradox," "character," and "setting". While working through your own inquiry one essays, consider how rhetorical tools (like those learned in English 111) could be useful when analyzing your texts. How might rhetorical terminology and literary analysis terminology overlap? How can we use these close reading skills to critically understand texts that may not be deemed "literature" such as music videos, song lyrics, commercials, articles, etc.?

Soft Rain on a Hot Mind

Maisie Laud

Writer's Reflection

This inquiry concept was, at first, very hard for me to grasp. I wanted to sort of, 'barf up,' all the knowledge I had acquired about Ray Bradbury, the atomic bomb, the context of the story, and my previous experience reading this story in addition to The Martian Chronicles. So at first, I sort of just jotted down all that knowledge and tried to present an representation of what I took from the story. Upon closer analysis, including rereading the story as well as reading previous Inquiry 1's in the CCM, I tried to digest the story from a different standpoint. I had originally tried to write a summary of the story in comparison to its World War II context, which was not the intent of Inquiry 1. So...I slept on it. I still couldn't figure out how I wanted to portray my take of the story, so I chose a quote from the story that spoke to me in a way that I could incorporate my previous knowledge of the context as well as develop an entirely new standpoint for the literary analysis. I chose to write about the paranoia of the story, its audience, and the time period, which proved to be, in my opinion, a good way to join my background with the story with a newly developed and coherent analysis of the audience.

My analysis is intended, primarily, for a class that is studying either the atomic bomb, or science-fiction writing. I would hope that my analysis sort of clues the readers into a different way of approaching a story, especially in dealing with a sensitive topic such as World War II. Basically, what I want my audience to get from this piece is a clear idea as to how people where influenced by this story in a post-atomic era. After the closing paragraph, I want them to say, "oh, well that does make sense."

Since it started off pretty rough, and I was unaware of what was required, this analysis proved to be somewhat difficult. Since I had previously read the story, I just wanted to say everything that previous teachers had told me about the story, and I'd just hand it in and get an A. But, upon writing the memo and receiving comments back, I realized that this wasn't the way to get an A, and if I want an

A, I'd have to do my own work on developing a well thought out analysis of the story, which is, what I did.

My analysis is significant because I think it dissects an overlooked concept of writing: the audience.

◆ ◆ ◆

Paranoia seeds from factual history- the fear that if something previously happened, it has the ability to happen again. Ray Bradbury takes this sensitive aspect, specifically the paranoia that arose in post-World War II America, and is able to capture an audience by creating a similar atmosphere in his science-fiction story There Will Come Soft Rains. He uses vague yet vivid visuals such as a destroyed city that gave off a radioactive glow and literary devices such as creating a story in media res to set off a war in the minds of the readers. The power of the human mind to create the worst possible scenario is incredible. The emotional response to Bradbury's vivid imagery, such as the radioactive glow from the city that seems to have just suffered some great catastrophe, allows the reader himself to create an entire disaster of a backstory from what little detail we are given about the context.

Bradbury's use of atomic imagery holds the audience in an uncomfortable state. If the reader is able to connect an image with previous knowledge, such as the atomic bomb, the result is an uncomfortable paranoia. He describes mid-way through the story that, "at night, the ruined city gave off a radioactive glow, which could be seen for miles" (Bradbury 1). Immediately, one's mind thinks of some green glow coming from a destroyed city far off in the distance. Bradbury forces the readers to create their own backstory with the clues given in the story, but without writing anything. He manipulates the audience through a hidden subtext. By starting the story after a significant event, he creates a mental game that forces the audience to decide their own backstory. During the time of the atomic bombings in 1945, Americans were brutally aware of the consequences of an atomic bomb. Words like "radiation "and "atomic," and phrases like "air raid," "fall-out shelter," and "weapons of mass destruction" became day-to-day words, and their definitions held harsh connotations. We are left with a visual familiar to our comprehension of an atomic bomb but are left to create our own story about what happened to the city, for Bradbury does not tell us.

Ray Bradbury starts off the sentence with "at night"(1), leaving the reader with a dark yet blank image for Bradbury to draw upon. "At night," refers to when no one can see anything, almost literally leaving the reader in the dark. Today's society feels the need to be "in the know" of everything. As an audience, we are manipulated by something we have not even read yet. We have this urgency to be aware of all of our surroundings at any given moment, and Bradbury takes that away from us, as readers. Bradbury uses this kind of writing technique to keep the readers in the dark, because keeping information from an audience can make them uncomfortable. For years people have been afraid of the dark because they cannot see what is going on, and Bradbury uses that to promote the paranoia of the reader that he is creating.

The words "ruined city"(1) leave the audience thinking about the possibility of a natural disaster, or maybe a war. What does that entail? We don't know, but our minds jump to the conclusion we are most familiar with in the context of the story: warfare. We are left to come up with backstory ourselves. Whenever there is a lack of information, we, as readers, become terribly uncomfortable and create our own information from the given clues. As a society, we jump to conclusions, and we base those conclusions off, generally speaking, paranoid assumptions for the worst possible conclusion. The story seems nearly innocent enough for the readers to develop an entire backstory of their own. By not even writing a backstory to the story, Bradbury inadvertently and subconsciously forces the audience to come up with their own.

The next phrase after his description of the city is that it "gave off a radioactive glow"(1). The "radioactive glow" (1) points to a word that the audience is unfortunately aware of: atomic. That word held an entire population paranoid of an impending counter-attack in the wake of World War II. The term paranoia seeds from suspicion of any possible outcome based on prior knowledge. The prior knowledge to the story was the ever-so-recent world war, and leaves the audience wondering if Bradbury was actually writing a story with the possibility of it being the reaction to a possible nuclear attack, or was just writing a post-apocalypse sci-fi story. But right here, the story clicks for the paranoid reader: this futuristic place has been hit with something radioactive, and the resulting radioactivity hums around the destroyed city with impending potentiality. Its eeriness captures the reader and makes them think of the previous historical context (that of the atomic bomb) in which the story is being written, and the suspicion builds.

A dark industrial silhouette defines the setting of a city, an image that could be "seen for miles"(1). Clearly, the words that Bradbury uses are not a coincidence. The rest of the story takes place in this abandoned house, where clearly something has destroyed a population, but we, as readers, create the rest of the plot in our heads, and our minds jump to conclusions. The far off city is the thing that has been hit, but whatever has happened has clearly affected their entire surrounding areas, for the house itself is abandoned. It creates a mental war within our minds between over thinking and basing our own ideas on previous knowledge as a means of learning from our mistakes. This shows that all paranoia spurs from the mind.

Given the post-World War II context, Ray Bradbury has taken an already tenderly uncomfortable audience and given them a story that plays with their heads, without even writing anything terribly specific. This specific quote not only captures an image in the mind of the reader, but also makes the reader question the theme and surrounding context. As readers, we want to know everything, but Bradbury does not give us enough. In fact, Bradbury gives us a template in which we must draw our own conclusions, creating a war within our own minds as to what is happening and what happened before the story.

Editorial Team's Note

Maisie Laud's close reading of Ray Bradbury's science-fiction story not only demonstrates how to closely read a very small section of text, but also reveals the power of word choice and context. Instead of merely summarizing the story and comparing that summary to the World War II context, Laud takes her analysis one step further by closely examining how a single sentence helps set the tone for the entire story. She pays close attention to the connotations of certain words and phrases, such as "radiation" and "air raid," and determines that those words and phrases would have created a sense of paranoia in Bradbury's post-war audience. Her argument is both specific and focused, in that she frames the essay around the one sentence that she is analyzing, breaking it down slowly for the reader and examining each word or phrase individually in terms of the story's World War II context. As you begin practicing your own close readings, consider how you might examine key words or phrases from a text to help add to your analysis. How might you determine which words/phrases are worth analyzing? What kind of contexts, such as the historical context that Laud picks up on here, might affect your close readings? Laud also plays close attention to audience (both her own and the source text's) throughout the essay. How might audience come into play as you conduct your close readings?

Inquiry Two:
Cultural and Historical Analysis

Though this year's print *CCM* is highlighting only Part B of Inquiry Two, we urge you to visit our online supplement to view the Part A work that goes with these essays.

America the Beautiful?

Beasy Jennison

Writer's Reflection

After finishing my inquiry two essay, a research essay about The Americans and how the process of "projection" helps to explain the negative reviews given by Americans of the time period, I am proud to say that I accomplished many goals. In doing this essay I managed my time extremely wisely, I organized my essay not only so that it flowed, but also to avoid the standard five paragraph essay, and I explored my vocabulary and voice. Each of these feats were difficult and things that I personally wanted to develop and grow on as a writer. In regards to my time management, I found that with this essay I paced myself extraordinarily well. Usually, I am the typical student who waits until the last minute to "pop out" a sub-par essay. However, this time around, I worked on this essay many days before hand, even during spring break. When I had free time around my dorm, I would make the goal to do one paragraph of my essay. Through this I was able to get my essay done and not simply submit, but edit and redo parts of a draft. Another notable mention about my inquiry two essay is my organization. Partially due to the amount of time I had to work on this essay, given the time allotted by the professor and my improved management of time, I was able to explore different ways to organize my paper. I was able to read it through many times and move paragraphs to aid in the "flow" of the overall piece. I think that I did a really good job and I think this may be one of the most organized essays I have ever written, which is exciting because I have always struggled with organization. And finally, because I had a lot of time to work on this essay, I got a chance to experiment with my voice and vocabulary. I didn't want to change my voice, but I did want to attempt to improve it. Strengthen my vocabulary and add larger words, without sounding pretentious. I think I succeeded in this in that my essay still sounds like me, but I managed to incorporate better words and wording.

◆ ◆ ◆

"A slashing and bitter attack on U.S. institutions"; "A Degradation of a Nation!"; "a sad poem for sick people"(Lane). This is only a small sampling of the negative reviews ensuing from the publishing of Robert Franks, *The Americans*. Upon the release of *The Americans* in The United States, the country was propelled into a "flying frenzy", offended and fuming from the audacious material captured forever in film. Yet this book was first released in Paris, France and was not only a popular buy, but was exalted as innovative and inspiring art. How and why can a book, pervaded with the same images, be so contrarily viewed? The process "projection", in which human beings interpret, relate, and respond to photos, and the repressed denial felt by Americans faking the "cookie cutter" ideal of 1950s America, offers insight and a possible solution as to why the American retort is exponentially more cross than the reactions of other countries.

The Swiss born Robert Frank came to America in 1947, arriving in the well-known city of New York, New York.

He had an idea and dream, applied for a loan, and set off on his journey of unveiling the truth of life in America. Robert Frank wanted to venture on the roads of America with only his camera, observing and documenting the raw, unedited citizens within. He didn't have them pose in any specific way, nor did he stage any scene. He merely saw and snapped.

Frank took over twenty-seven thousand pictures as he zigzagged from coast to coast. From the original twenty-seven thousand, he managed to narrow down to only one thousand pictures those he felt were successful in portraying the "true" America. Clearly, one thousand pictures are too enormous for one book and publishing this many photos would be detrimental to the overall impact of his work. This being said, he then "spread them across the floor of his studio and tacked them to the walls for a final edit. Out of a year and a half of work, Frank chose just 83 images" (Cole). These eighty-three photos, bearing a one-sentence caption of a title, place, and date, revealed America in a light never seen before, or at least a light that until then had remained ignored. From cover to cover, *The Americans* ensnared not only the faces of strangers, but he put on film the unspoken plights of The United States, the racial tensions segregating the country, and the obligatory stereotypes of the 1950s.

Retrospectively, the 1950s are regarded as prosperous times. Posters and T.V. shows portrayed the lives of this decade as homely, sweet, and structured. Women had their "belonged" places in the kitchen and homes and were leaving the workforce, men were returning from war, back into the swing of a day-to-day job, the wealthy were relocating to the suburbs, crowded with the common "cookie cutter" houses of the decade. Everything was great...or so they chose to believe. This conception, this fantasy, polluted the minds of America, filling it with the illusion that one must fit this stereotype. Anyone or anything different was swept "under the rug" and their existence was ignored. As our banner proudly boasts, we are the "land of the free", we are America and proud. Our reputable reputation was vital and treasured.

With the cold war, not only was fear brought to our country, but competition as well. As one source states, "1945 marked the beginning of the Cold War. With this came the increased emphasis on consumerism and physical attractiveness in the United States. We began to produce more consumer goods and believed we had "better looking", "feminine" women than Russia. The ideology of the Cold War had an important impact on U.S domesticity, affecting such things as the design of suburban houses to relations between the sexes...the baby boom and feminine mystique were direct responses to the Cold War and to the anxieties it created" (Salvino). America didn't strive for mediocrity, as a people they strove to be the best. However, America had its predicaments, whether they were acknowledged or not. One-fifth of the United States, a population of 150,697,361 citizens, was living under the poverty line; meaning 30,139,473 people were living day-to-day trying to simply get by (U.S. Census Bureau). With the majority of the population craving to keep the image of America ideal, they chose to remain ignorant to these citizens and their very presence. Until Robert Frank opened their eyes to the very truth they tried to conceal.

In view of the fact that *The Americans* was published in the 1950s, it is simple for one to speculate the reason for why this book made the impact it did. As stated previously, the 1950s were changing times and physical appearance and staying in the "norm" of the time was vital in order to have acceptance. Researchers do not struggle to connect events such as these to explain *The Americans* and the reactions it arose. The anger explicitly expressed is due to Americans seeing for the first time what they elected not to see. However, this is just the tip of an iceberg of research that could be done.

One cannot simply take hostilities and happenings from the time period and use them to elucidate the negative feedback from Americans towards this book. Although that is a part of the explanation, its compulsory to explore and study photojournalism and how people interpret photos to better understand how occurrences in the1950s played a part in the infamous American reviews. A book called *Photojournalism: Principles and Practices*, by Keith P. Sanders, goes into detail about the approach to photo interpretation in relation to *The Americans*. Sanders suggests that "What a photograph 'means' to a person is the result of a complex interaction between the photograph and the person's prior experiences and perceptions." (Sanders 126). This process that Sanders addresses is referred to as "projection". To put this concept simply, "projection" is where a person subconsciously uses past experiences, sensations, and thoughts to interpret and react to ambiguous photos, such as those represented in *The Americans*. This act of "projection" is frequently used in a psychological test termed the Thematic Apperception Test. This test, originally done by psychologists and students at the Harvard Psychological Clinic(Frey 2001), where people are shown ambiguous photos and told to write for ten minutes in order to create a story of what is going on in the photo. After the examination, the individuals were asked questions about their past experiences and memories. People who responded negatively to these photos tended to voice that they didn't have any negative experiences relating to the subject matter displayed, but after some "digging" researchers found that the subconscious of these individuals reveals repressed negativity, directly related to these photos, repressed by the brain.

This act of "projection" adds a new element to research about the work of Robert Frank. As opposed to stating that the correlation between the events of the time period and the rejection to this book is a direct result from the negativity surrounding the states, one should think of it more as Americans subconsciously channeling the distresses of the decade, evoked by the pictures from Robert Frank. Americans were living in a "perfect" world to help cope with the drama of the world and to exert the beauty of our country. Once Robert Frank revealed the overlooked aspects of the country to its residents, suppressed anger and rage was unleashed in forms of venomous reviews. Perhaps "America the Beautiful" was not as "beautiful" as once assumed.

Works Cited

"1950 United States Census." *Wikipedia.* Wikimedia Foundation, 03 Jan. 2013. Web. 12 Mar. 2013.

Cole, Tom. "'Americans': The Book That Changed Photography." NPR. NPR, 14 Feb. 2009. Web. 3 Mar. 2013.

Frey, Rebecca J. "Thematic Apperception Test." Encyclopedia of Mental Disorders. N.p.,n.d. Web. 16 Mar. 2013.

Lane, Anthony. "Road Show." Editorial. The New Yorker 14 Sept. 2009: n. pag. *The New Yorker.* 14 Sept. 2009. Web. 13 Mar. 2013.

Salvino, Bianca. "1950-1960." 1950-1960. N.p., n.d. Web. 11 Mar. 2013.

Sanders, Keith P. "Research in Photojournalism," in Cliftin C Edom, *Photojournalism: Principles and Practices* (Dubuque William C. Brown. 1976). p. 126

Henry A. Murray, *Explorations in Personality.* (New York: John Wiley and Sons. 1938). p. 531

Frank, Robert. *The Americans.* Gottingen: Steidl, 2008..

Editorial Team's Note

In this effective cultural/historical Analysis, Beasy Jennison offers an insightful analysis of a visual text by examining its reception during the time and place in which it was created. By looking at the historic and cultural context of 1950s America, Jennison notes why the work of Robert Franks might have been so negatively received in one location, despite its positive reviews in other countries. In addition to providing an astute research-based analysis of the psychology of a nation within a particular cultural/historic context, Jennison's work is organized and focused, offering an effective argument that flows and transitions well throughout. This paper also brings up questions that may be applied to other contexts: How are values defined by a culture in a particular time and place? In what ways might norms be critiqued or analyzed? How might this provide a means of interrogating other works that are negatively – even violently – received within their cultural/historic setting?

PICTURES SHOWING TRUE
AMERICA STARTLE
"BEAUTIFUL" AMERICANS

Class Divide in the Hunger Games and American Society

Brian H. Jong

Writer's Reflection

We are all passengers aboard a colossal ship christened the S.S.C United States. Our hopes and aspirations rest upon this vessel as we sail through uncharted water to lands unknown. However, after numerous years of arduous voyage and unfavorable living conditions, a small group of passengers has grown progressively unruly and restless. They solicit the help of the ship's captain who allows the group to migrate to the upper deck so that they may enjoy the spectacular view and cool sea breeze. He proposes to erect facilities and accommodations for the group's enjoyment. The rest of the passengers are forced to relocate down to the lower decks in order to accommodate the group's desires. This ensues in massive overpopulation of the lower decks, causing the ship's foundations to be increasingly weakened, and cracks and fractures to emerge in its hull. Meanwhile, members of the group are spread out on poolside lounge chairs, enjoying the light breeze and warm sunshine, unceremoniously sipping coconut water from a bright yellow straw. They have been blinded by the surrounding comfort and luxury, unwittingly developing a dispassionate attitude towards the "cellar-dwellers". This has caused them to become completely oblivious to the impending chaos and doom amassed beneath their feet.

The short story that I composed above provides an apt representation of the increasingly fragmented nature of contemporary society in the United States. An undesirable trend has developed within American society where the population has been divided into distinct classes based on each individual's economic prowess. Over the years, the income gap between the upper and the lower classes has grown exponentially, leading to unrest among the lower classes who claim that they are constantly subjected to oppression from the upper classes. In my essay, I attempted to construct a relationship between the class warfare that Suzanne Collins portrayed in her novel, _The Hunger Games_, and the highly divisive state of American society today.

Personally, I found the research process to be the most challenging aspect of the essay. Due to the relative youthfulness in the publication date of the novel, the collection of scholarly articles available that addressed how the dystopian society depicted in it mirrored that of American society today was greatly limited. The few that I was able to find were inappropriate for application to the context of my argument. It turned out that only one of my sources actually bore a relation to both the novel and my argument. The other sources that I used were articles and abstracts from books and research papers that offered information regarding the income inequality in the United States, the disparities in power between the classes and the stereotypes that have been enacted by the upper classes towards the lower classes. I had to critically analyze the individual sources and develop a method to assimilate the information offered into the context of my argument. This process significantly encumbered my writing progress as there were numerous occasions when I would be forced to replace a source because its context was deviating away from the perimeters of my argument.

Although the research process was no doubt challenging, I felt that I have learned some interesting things from it. It was intriguing to discover that *The Hunger Games* was published on the day before the collapse of the Lehman Brothers. The research process also allowed me to gain a greater appreciation for the state of American society today where the trend of the lower classes being increasingly oppressed by the upper classes is prevalent. I also recognized the importance of starting the research process early in order to allow for sufficient time to judge the credibility, reliability and relevance of the sources.

Overall, Inquiry 3 is a greatly illuminating writing project that has enriched me in both my close reading and research abilities.

◆ ◆ ◆

In *The Hunger Games*, Suzanne Collins illustrates a desolate world where survivors of the post- apocalyptic North American continent of Panem are segregated into twelve separate districts and tasked with specific responsibilities of harvesting the Earth's remaining natural resources. The districts are subjected to the cruel oppression and exploitation by the continent's governing body, the Capitol, which exerts its sphere of influence over them through the employment of a tyrannical dictatorial regime, the keystone of which is the Hunger Games. In the novel, Collins highlights the contrast between the poverty and destitution experienced by the inhabitants of the districts, and the wealth and power possessed by the ruling class residing in the Capitol, detailing a futuristic dystopia civilization that is characterized by class warfare and bears an uncanny semblance to the highly divisive nature of American society today.

The novel was published on September 14, 2008, coincidentally the day before the Lehman Brothers filed for bankruptcy and exacerbated the already severe economic downturn in the United States. At the time of reading, many middle and lower class Americans were being confronted with the unappealing prospect of unemployment, making them more predisposed in identifying with the novel's dominant theme of oppression from the upper elite class. Suggestions about the prevalence of class warfare in American society were rampant during this period of time and protests were demonstrated by the 2011 organization of the Occupy Wall Street Movement that targeted social issues such as income inequality, greed, corruption and oppression by the upper elite classes. The movement aimed to "fight back against the richest 1% of people that are writing the rules of an unfair global economy that is foreclosing on our future" (Occupy Wall Street). The state of American society as described by proponents of the movement mirrors the severe income inequalities and unfairness inherent in the society portrayed by Collins in *The Hunger Games*. Collins' depiction of class warfare thus provides an apt reflection of the increasingly fragmented societal culture which has become an abominable quality of contemporary American society.

The vast economic disparity present in the United States has given rise to the formation of distinct classes in our society. Robert Hughes Jr. and Maureen Perry- Jenkins identified them to be the capitalist, upper middle, middle, working, working poor and underclass classes (177). Members of the upper capitalist class make up only one percent of the population while the other classes constitute the remaining ninety nine percent (Hughes, Perry Jenkins). A burgeoning income gap has developed between the two groups as a result of the simultaneous concentration of wealth and power in the hands of the economic elites and the deterioration in the living standards of the lower classes. David Harvey describes this trend as "an endeavor to restore class power to the richest strata in the population" (28). Overall economic wealth has not increased within the population. Rather, the unidirectional transfer of wealth from the lower classes to the upper capitalist class has allowed the latter to enjoy a larger slice of the economic pie (Harvey), thus widening the gap between the two classes. John Fund supports this argument by noting that in the United States, the majority of this "wealth and power seems to gravitate towards the Beltway and its suburbs" (Fund). He cites a survey conducted by Money Magazine that "looked at the 3,033 counties in the US and found that the top one-half of 1 percent is dominated by Washington, DC" (Fund).

The accumulation of immense wealth often corresponds to the possession of colossal power. This has become a characteristic of the upper capitalist class in our society today. Many of the politicians in Washington DC who are responsible for the most important decisions of the country belong to the upper capitalist class. The lower classes are severely underrepresented in the political arena as they are often labeled as unqualified to lead. Michael Zweig argues that "class must be understood in terms of power" (Zweig). His argument mirrors the vast power disparity between the upper capitalist class and the lower classes in our society today.

In *The Hunger Games*, the Capitol's residents and the district dwellers are the novel's equivalent of the upper capitalist class and the lower classes in American society respectively. The wealth and power disparity between both parties is exceedingly conspicuous. In the novel, Collins portrays the Capitol as the epitome of success and eminence. When Katniss, the novel's main protagonist, first arrived in the Capitol, she could not help but remark that:

> The cameras haven't lied about its grandeur. If anything they have not quite captured the magnificence of the glistening buildings in a rainbow of hues that tower into the air, the shiny cars that roll down the wide paved streets, the oddly dressed people with bizarre hair and painted faces who have never missed a meal. (Collins 59)

The "glistening buildings that tower in the air" appear to be a reference towards the numerous skyscrapers that adorn the skyline of many of America's metropolitan cities. The construction of these buildings would require a substantial amount of economic input. Thus, their presence in the Capitol serves to highlight the abundance of wealth that it possesses. The height of these buildings can also be interpreted as a symbol of the Capitol's power and authority over the districts. It articulates the hierarchical structure in Panem where the Capitol rests at the pinnacle of civilization while the districts are stranded at the bottom. Collins further emphasizes the wealth of the Capitol by describing the eccentric appearances (at least from Katniss' perspective) adorned by its citizens. The superficiality of the citizens demonstrates the vast amount of financial resources which they possessed, as well as their ostentatious consumption practices.

The districts, especially the higher numbered ones, are rendered by Collins as grim habitations characterized by starvation and misery. Katniss describes her district as "District 12. Where you can starve to death in safety" (Collins, 6). Each of the districts was tasked with the specific responsibility of fabricating a particular resource for the Capitol's consumption. For example, District 1 was tasked with the production of precious gems and stones, District 3 specialized in electronics, District 11 focused on agriculture and District 12 was responsible for the mining of coal (Collins). The Capitol exerted a monopolistic control over all of the resources produced without awarding fair compensation to the districts for their role in the production process. The unfair trading practice resulted in a huge wealth disparity between the districts and the Capitol, mirroring the arguments made by Harvey about the accumulation of wealth by the ruling elites at the expense of the lower classes. In this respect, Collins' depiction of the unequal wealth and resources distribution in Panem is a reflection of the widening income gap and power disparity in the United States that is a major contributing factor towards the increasing fragmentation of American society.

The division of American society into social classes has also inevitably given rise to class discrimination that is represented by the development of popular stereotypes towards expected behavioral patterns of the different classes in society. Paul Piff explains that: "facets of social class shape the identity of upper and lower class individuals and, like other social identity constructs (e.g. ethnicity and nation of origin), influence an individual's life circumstances and patterns of social perception and construal" (Piff, 2). The stereotypes are often enacted by the ruling class which "defines its goals and means not only for itself but for the whole society" (Skliar, 517). This means that based on its higher position in the class hierarchy, the ruling class has the power to enact classifications for the entire community without the consult of the lower classes. The establishment of stereotypes can be "a source of social stigma and rejection among individuals from lower class backgrounds" (Piff, 2). It could be interpreted by the lower classes as oppression from the upper class which could lead to social unrest, thus exacerbating the division in society.

Class discrimination in *The Hunger Games* was best symbolized by the character of Effie Trinket. Effie worked as the escort for the District 12 Hunger Games competitors and was a resident of the wealthy and powerful Capitol. She was a member of the upper echelon of the hierarchal system in Panem who had never experienced the suffering that characterized the living standards in the districts. Therefore, her knowledge of the districts was limited to the censored propaganda that the Capitol disseminated and her observations of the tributes whom she escorted to the Capitol each year.

Her ignorance was highlighted when she made a rather condescending remark to both Katniss and Peeta during supper on the Capitol bound train that "at least you two have decent manners" (Collins, 44). She continued by describing the previous year's tributes as "a couple of savages" (Collins, 44) whose lack of table manners had upset her digestion. Her supercilious comment showed that she did not think highly of the inhabitants of the districts. She had formulated an ill-informed opinion towards the behavior of the inhabitants of the districts that was based on a superficial understanding of the circumstances which had led to the kind of behavior displayed by the tributes. Her upbringing in a life of privilege had given her a superiority complex that she innately believed gave her the authority to cast judgments towards the appropriateness of certain types of behavior.

Effie further exemplifies the persona of class stereotyping during her attempts to win Katniss and Peeta sponsors in which she tries to communicate their successful "struggle to overcome the barbarism of your district" (Collins, 74) as an attractive proposition for sponsors to invest in. Her impulsive use of the word "barbarism" to describe the society of District 12 implies a form of arrogance and aloofness that she believed was afforded to her by the position that she occupied at the top rung of the class hierarchy in Panem. In response to her insensitive comment, Katniss discreetly commented, "Barbarism? That's ironic coming from a woman helping to prepare us for slaughter. And what's she basing our success on? Our table manners?" (Collins, 74). Katniss was clearly frustrated by the unreasonable amount of oppression and stereotyping that she was consistently being targeted with by the citizens of the Capitol. Effie's discriminatory attitude towards District 12 is thus a befitting reflection of the upper class' casting of stereotypes that have contributed to the increased marginalization of the lower classes in contemporary American society.

Society in the United States has also been divided such that each class has specific roles and responsibilities within the community. The capitalist, upper middle and middle classes are usually identified with a service based industry that offers moderate to high wages with working benefits. On the other hand, the working, working poor and underclass classes are often associated with labor intensive jobs with low wages and poor working conditions (Hughes, Perry Jenkins). The occupational system reflected in *The Hunger Games* bears similarities to contemporary US society. In the novel, the Capitol has a service based industry where the primary focus of the citizens was consumption. The intensiveness of labor would increase from the lower to the higher numbered districts, mirroring contemporary American society in which the lower classes usually perform the most labor intensive work. Income is often awarded disproportionately to the amount of labor performed. Workers with a more labor intensive line of work often earn a lower income compared to employees with a more service based line of work. This inequality in the designation of income is a key contributing factor towards the divisive nature of American society that is also related to the argument presented earlier regarding the widening income gap between the upper capitalist and lower classes.

There are members of American society who fervently deny the existence of class disparities in the United States. However, those claims have proven falsified, evidenced by the wealth and power divergence between the upper and lower classes, class discrimination, and the installation of specific roles and responsibilities for members of society. Class disparities have undoubtedly become both a valid and worrying concern in contemporary American society. While our society has certainly not degenerated to the extent of Panem, the undesirable components which it exhibits nevertheless possess the potential to undermine the values of democracy and liberty that have long been vaunted as the unshakeable pillars of American society. If these negative components in our society remain unattended, they could steer the United States on a path that is branded by oppression

and exploitation by the upper capitalist class. It is irrefutable that the
Hunger Games are right at our doorstep.

Works Cited

"About Us" Occupy Wall Street. n.p.n.d. Web. 29 Mar. 2013 Hughes,
    Robert Jr, Perry-Jenkins, Maureen. "Social Class Issues in
    Family Education". National Council on Family Relations.
    JSTOR. Web. 29 Mar. 2013

Collins, Suzanne. "The Hunger Games", September 2009. Scholastic
    Press. Print. 29 Mar. 2012

Fund, John. "The One Percenters' Fortress City." The American Spec
    tator. 45.5, p 58, 2012. Literature Resource Center. Web. 29
    Mar. 2013

Harvey, David. "Neoliberalism as Creative Destruction." American
    Academy of Political and Social Science, 2007. JSTOR. Web. 29
    Mar. 2013

Piff, Paul. "On Wealth and Wrongdoing: How Social Class Affects
    Unethical Behavior". University of California, Berkeley. Pro
    Quest LLC. Web. 29 Mar. 2013

Skliar, Leslie. "Social Movements for Global Capitalism: The Transna
    tional Capitalist Class of America." Taylor & Francis, Ltd.
    JSTOR. Web. 29 Mar. 2013

Zweig, Michael. "Six Points on Class". Monthly Review: An Inde pen
    dent Socialist Magazine, 2006. Academic Search Complete.
    Web. 29 Mar. 2013

Editorial Team's Note

In his Inquiry Two analysis, Brian Jong uses his research on the American class system as a lens for reading Suzanne Collins' *The Hunger
Games.* Jong provides extensive background information that allows
him to not only compare his source text (*The Hunger Games*) to that
information, but also to deepen his understanding of Collins' text as a
whole. Throughout the essay, the Jong examines specific details from
the source text that help him solidify his argument, such as the skyscrapers and the roles of each district. This strong analysis is aided by
the inclusion of counter-viewpoints, specifically those of people who
do not believe a class system exists in America. Acknowledging those
opposing viewpoints demonstrates that Jong has considered the issue

from multiple angles and has done extensive research (which helps establish his ethos as an author). As you compose your Inquiry 2 essay, what opposing viewpoints might be worth acknowledging as you make your argument? In addition, how might you use specific details from the source text, alongside your research, to help strengthen your overall argument?

Inquiry Three: Creative and Critical Application

Steubenville Rape Case Remix

Diana Konik

This project can be found on the *CCM* **Online**

I just want you to realize that I'm sorry.
I know I ruined her life, for life.

RAISING AMERICA | MA'LIK RICHMOND
CONVICTED OF RAPE

Writer's Reflection

Introduction:

When this inquiry was proposed to me, it was right after spring break and during break I was aware of the recent events that were occurring on the news, and the Steubenville rape case was one of the top stories that was being broadcasted. There were many different arguments about the case ranging anywhere from feminist groups protesting during the trial to people having sympathetic feelings for the two star football players. In the midst of all the different sides I created my own opinion about the conversation, therefore I knew right away that creating a remix was going to help me propel my argument to audiences. With the Steubenville rape case has the backbone to my remix, my main argument was that teen partying is an issue in America and parents of young teens need to be more involved in their child's life, so they are not influenced by peer pressure and making bad decisions that could ultimately destroy their future.

There are not any specific remix examples that I can pinpoint in which I wanted to imitate, that made me decide on how to create my own remix. I basically already knew how I wanted to create the remix, by mashing up clips of different news reports from different stations and leaked tweets, photos, and a cellphone video that was recorded the night of the incident. With this mash up I also decided to incorporate some Hollywood clips from the movies "Project X" and "Spring Breakers" to show an extreme case of teen partying, and also play the song "Young, Wild, and Free" by Snoop Dog.

From knowing how I wanted to make my remix, the definition that I chose for my remix would be the compilation and assemblage remix definition. This is taking a combination of already existing text and creating a new text, and this is exactly how I wanted to create my remix for this project. By making a combination of already existing text, the newscast stories and movies clips, I was able to build relationships between each video clip and provide an argument. Based on this definition, I would suppose an example of a remix that influenced me, would be the "You Can't Vote in Change" video that was shown in class. I thought this was the best definition for my project because of the resources that were available for to me to create the remix. The resources are the news stories from CNN and ABC that I found on YouTube, the previews of the movies, and the pictures from the case such as tweets. By combining these resources in an organized manner this helped me to develop an argument by creating a new text from a combination of already existing text.

Rhetorical Choices:

Working through the project, I was always thinking about the rhetorical choices that I was making and reasons as to why I was putting clips in a certain order, or why pictures would match with the words to the song. Therefore, going through the process of creating my remix everything that I did had no unintentional purpose; they were all intentional in order to make my argument more clear. I could go through the whole video and explain every little rhetorical reason as to why I made something a certain way, but I'll only focus on some of the broad aspects of the remix.

One of the first things that you might notice is the repetition of matching three different pictures with the words "young, wild, and free". For the first picture and first word, "young", each time I put a picture of the two boys to literally show that these were young teenagers that were involved in this case of teen partying. For the second picture and second word, "wild", I put the Instagram picture and the two pictures of profane tweets that were about the incident that occurred that night. This was to show how that these young teenagers were really being "wild" in a sense of posting terrible pictures and tweets on social media sites. The third picture and third word, "free", I matched a screen capture of a news article on the Internet about how the two boys were guilty, they had to register as sex offenders, and were sentenced to juvenile detention center. The reason for this set up was to show that at the time the young boys were partying and didn't care because they felt free, but now because of the poor choices they committed, they will not be free anymore. This is essentially an irony to show that these young teenagers may be young and they can be wild, but ultimately they must suffer the consequences for the decisions they made the night of the incident.

A second rhetorical choice that I made was repeating the movie clips that showed extreme partying that matched the hook of the song (The hook is the part of song where it starts out as "So what we get drunk, so what we smoke weed..."). I did this repetition only twice and on the last repeated hook, I added the protestors outside the courtroom during the trial. Repeating the extreme partying was to show that young teenagers are influenced by this movie fantasy of partying, and having fun with no parents around. In reality it is against the law to drink under age, and the only way that these teens are able to have alcohol at these fantasy parties is if their parents buy it for them. Then at the last hook I showed clips of the protestors to argue that the decision that not only these teens made but the parents made, led to national news and people literally protesting against the trial of the two accused boys.

One last rhetorical choice was that I added the leaked camera video that was made by a teenager videoing another teenager talking about the rape incident that occurred that night, and even talking about the two boys that were accused of sexual assault. I added clips from the leaked video in between clips from the news stories to show how the lawyers of the two boys and the Malik Richmond basically contradicted themselves in saying that there was no evidence that the young girl was incoherent the night of the incident, and that she did give consent to the alleged assaults. However, based on the leaked video it is clear that the teenage girl was very intoxicated that night because of the profane comments made by the teenage boy in the video saying that she was "dead". I wanted to show that adults were trying to find every possible way to make it seem like the two accused boys were innocent and did nothing wrong. However in reality, the question should be where were the parents to monitor these teenagers to make sure that this incident didn't occur or even the motion of caring about where their child was in the late hours of the night. My point is to show that not only were the accused guilty, but also everyone involved in the incident are guilty, including the parents. The parents made the decision to not to want to set boundaries, and allowed their child to run wild and not make good decision for themselves.

Rhetorical Velocity:

It is obvious that this remix video would be distributed on YouTube, because it is the easiest way to propel this remix into the public, so that other third parties can view the remix. From there it would be ideal for the video to be shared through social media sites such as Facebook or Twitter. The ideal time that I would have liked this video to be released would have been at the peak time of the trial (at the end of spring break), when it was being constantly shown on television, and the arguments and opinions were being discussed. Right now the Steubenville incident is on a downward slope, but other similar incidents that are occurring around the country are being revealed on the news, so releasing the video right now would still be appropriate. Thinking about how my remix could be redistributed by third parties, would probably be more for educational purposes. I'm thinking that the arguments that I portray can help back up another person's argument that may be related to the same topic. The combination of clips from the news stories and the leaked camera video could be used in another person's remix. It would be more likely that the argument that I present would be redistributed because it is different from the arguments about rape culture in America.

Looking back on the project, I really didn't have any difficulties in creating this project. I knew what I wanted to do from the very beginning; so creating the remix was relatively quite easy. Something that I do wish that I had was a more advanced iMovie on my computer. Having the basic iMovie limits you from doing certain editing functions on the video, but upgrading to a higher iMovie cost money, so I had to work with what I had. Overall, I think I did the best I could, and put in a lot of thought into the project in order for audiences to clearly understand the argument that I was portraying through this remix video.

Editorial Team's Note

View Diana Konik's video remix concerning the Steubenville rape case of 2012, **featured on the *CCM* website**, and consider her reflection. In her remix, Konik argues against the potentially dangerous outcomes of underage drinking through information circulated on the high profile Steubenville, Ohio rape case. Konik connects clips together carefully that provide conflicting information to show how easily information can be skewed by the media. Furthermore, Konik places emphasis on how skewed information can influence the public's opinion of the case, as referenced through screen captures of tweets and other social media posts. Konik uses several different modes of communication to provide her overall message on the Steubenville rape case and the public's reaction to it. Based on Konik's work and your own understanding of remixes, how would you define the term 're-mix'? In what ways did Konik attempt to persuade or influence her audience? How might you present a similar argument while using a different medium? How would your own work change based on your chosen medium?

How to Survive English 112 for International Students
Jia Yao Wang

Writer's Reflection

When I was thinking of my inquiry three, I thought it should be my last assignment for the English 112 course. Before taking this English 112 course, I had already dropped it last semester. So I created a short story based on the talking with my friends and their English 112 experiences. When I created the story, it was definitely hard for me to repeat all the information on people talking. Also it has background plots, detailed information and motivation for me to write for each individual person. More than that, I had to cover the time line of a whole semester, to make sure the story is complete, informative and easy to understand. The purpose for the essay is expressing that English 112 is tough for international students.

After I finished my draft, my classmates give me valuable advice about my essay. My essay contains obvious grammar issues many times. I went to my English workshop studio and asked my teacher, he gave feedback on my essay and it helped me a lot on the grammar, structure and creative part. He said I should give more detail information about each character, to let the reader know how to distinguish them. A story should be close to real life but not real life, so it can be expressed as comedy, horror, and romantic etc. For this reason, I have created the plots to full fill the body of my story. In addition to the creative part and the grammar issues, he also gave a list for the translation in each individual paragraph. Through appropriate translation, it was very convincing for me to edit the essay for fluency. After class my studio teacher talked with my 112 teacher about my essay, and he said my ideas are very smart. As international students, English is not our mother language, so it is hard for English 112 teachers to help us, since most of the students in class are American students, they do not need to guide the basic errors like grammar and format.

This is how I added new sources in my essay. First when I changed the genre from dialogue to short story, I wanted my characters alive not dead. So I added detail information to describe personal appearances and background information to let the reader know the story is real. Similarly an attractive story should have transition for the plot for different persons, such as dropping class in the midterm. In this short story, I collected four different personal individual stories, and put them together into one new story. They knew each other before, but I also added other students' story in my essay, which makes it more informative and worth to read. I do not want my story talking about English 112 one course during the time line, so what I did is expanding the line to be complex and close to university life. I think school life is not only assignments and exams but also it has love stories, parties and a variety of entertainment.

Before I wrote the essay, I asked each person individually, if they could give me the opportunity to write their story on my essay but without real names. My friends told me it is ok, and if it is possible they want to be different in the story, such as they hope the character is more handsome, taller and smart. I told them it is fine, I will try my best to make the story worth reading. But most of them just do not want to be the bad guy in the story, I can understand.

I think during my creative story I learned how to expand the story and it is feels goods for me. I had to organize the story with a process map, which is the first step and which is the second step. Later I followed the time line to expand the story, it just like you follow the cook book to make cake, everything should follow the process. And finally I had to make it by myself, change the formula for the cake, which makes it more attractive. When I finished my inquiry three essay, my teacher suggested me to publish it for the CCM. I never thought I could be a good writer in English since I have bad memories about English 112 before. But now, I think I need to revise my paper and talk with my English teacher about it. If my essay is published, I think it is a good way to educate me and keep me writing in the future. Maybe I am not expert in writing, but writing brings me happiness which I never have had before.

◆ ◆ ◆

In Miami University, there are four Chinese students living in one dorm their freshman year. Now it is the time for them to select their courses for next semester. They have different last names, respectively, Zack, Jonny, Hegel and Li. According to school policy on selecting courses, each of them has a different time to select the course, but they were planning to take same Miami Plan course, which makes it easy for them to prepare for the exam together. Basically most of the Miami Plan courses are not your major course, they require you know basic information in one liberal area. Jonny and Zack study computer engineering, and they have same height but different shape on their body; Zack has played basketball for ten years; he is in the school basketball club. And Jonny's hobby is video games, when we watched the live matches, he did not watch the game no matter if it has a player representing China. Hegel enjoys reading books and movies, and he downloads movies and e-books all free from the Internet even though he knows it is illegal in America. Li is fond of finance; he had his personal EBay selling goods in both America and China. Most of the time, he does not want to miss the selling time on websites, so he made two clock for himself. One is scheduling the time for class, group meeting and his part time job, the other is for the discount time on different websites.

It was nine o'clock on Saturday night, they chatted about selecting their courses. They checked rate my professor, GPA distribution for the professor and found available times for themselves. Only Li did not care about the GPA distribution, he said. He thought different people took the same course, so the distribution cannot directly tell us if the course is hard or easy. It was said by Zack "I am the last one to select my courses, but I definitely need to take English 112 this semester, do you want to take the same course with me?" Jonny turn off the music on his mac and said, "I think it is ok, but I know some of junior students from China, they told me English 112 is very tough for international students. Before you take the course, you had better to check the professor is easy or not." After that Hegel replied to Jonny: "I know this website, it is kind of helpful for the American students. As it based on the statistics information by American students, maybe it's not suitable for us to select the professor? I think we should ask the junior students, they might have taken it before. What you folks think?"

All of them nodded their head, so Hegel chatted with the junior students on the Facebook. After a few minutes, he told them there was no easy way to find an easy course for English 112. The majority of the courses are taught by graduate students in English department, in Miami. Further none of them have the same themes. Someone played movies; others read novels and even required playing a game and write reflections. Even if you know the teacher's name, you cannot find the information on rate my professor. Then Jonny said: "So even if we knew it is easy teacher; we still did not know his or her theme for this semester? I just do not understand, why we need to take it? I do not understand, why it is a requirement in Miami plan not for me but for the American students." Li got off his phone and said: "For now, we do not have better options. I think we should select different courses in the first week, so we will have one week to consider which professor is easy to pass this course?" Li finished eating the burger on his hand, and turned back to watch his TV show on the laptop.

Everyone agreed with Li's idea, so they selected four different professors for English 112. After the first week taking the courses, they were too busy on their own so they forget to talk about the schedule or course. They forget to meet and decided to take whose course. Li had to take care of his girlfriend. Hegel was coding on his laptop for his computer science course, Zack was training with basketball team members in gym. Later he would play a half semester basketball competition for his club. The plan they thought in the beginning of the semester, was already forgotten by them.

After a month, Li realized they forget to discuss the same 112-course plan, but it was too late for them to be in same course together. On Friday night Li spoke to everyone in the dorm: "I definitely know, we forgot the112 plan. But I could not change the course, my girlfriend forced me to do it. In my112 courses, I had to read three novels and I had never heard before and we had one quiz every two weeks. I have to say, I had tried my best on reading, as the quiz always ask me specific questions. 'What is the color of is leading male character's shoes?' or 'What is the quote by the artisan?' It was hard for me to read the book, but he requires more than that. I hate reading, every time I had to read over twenty pages for the quiz." Jonny stepped inside the room and said: "Oh lucky for you! If you take my course, you will not only hate reading but also hate watching movies. During the course time, we have to watch several movie trailers, and we have to talk about what the director wants to say in the movie. After we discuss the movie trailer, we have to write a reflection about the trailer. You know, I cannot find any subtitles for the movie. And sometimes, I had to watch the trailer again and again to understand the motivation, connection between different music."

Zack just came back from another university, he joined the conversation. "I had to say it was lucky for me for English 112. Our teacher requires me play a game called Diablo III, and write blogs about why designers set up the puzzle on the bridge, house or the bathroom. However, some of my friends in the basketball team had played it before. So it was not hard for me to write blogs on the puzzle design. How about your 112 it is easy or not, Hegel?"

Hegel dropped the headphone from his ears, then answered: "I did not know what to say about my 112, I had no require reading before class, which is easy for me. And I had no reflection or blog write after class, but I had to write blogs during class time. The theme for my class is American History, and I read the Chinese version of Franklin's autobiography before I came to America. More or less, I think it will help me a little bit to find appropriate topic to write."

After a month, all of them had main projects to work on. It was midnight on Sunday. Li, Hegel and Zack in the dorm, they were typing their assignment for 112.

Suddenly Li said: "Oh! My god. I just finished the reading part for the novel; I have to write at least five pages of paper for reflection of the novel. He told to himself in his mind, analyze the main character, and structure of the story. What's the author's main purpose of the paper?" He struggled, and had no idea in his head. So he tried to search the information on Google. But there was no relevant information about the novel, because the novel was published by Miami and wrote by one of the chairs in the English department in the 70s. He said, "I cannot write any more about this novel reflection." Hegel and Zack turned their head to Li, and said at same time, " Never give up". Then Hegel said, "Maybe you can work on other assignments for your class; you have to forget the 112 assignments in your head. Maybe when you came back, you'll have better ideas on it. We can have some food from the basement vending machine. How about that, Li?" Li replied: "Works for me. I am a little bit tired right now." So all of them had a break for about five minutes, but Li still have no idea on writing. Zack came back from regular training and told Li: " Li, you can try the Writing Center in King library. But you need to make an appointment before you come. And as I know, you need to select the instructor before you go. I suggested to select an instructor whose major is English, Communication, Education, or Philosophy. I know most of them have taken more advanced literature courses, and they have longer assignments than we do in 112." Li answered Zack back: "I know they give international students suggestions, and each appointment is around one hour. But they waste time on introducing each other and giving feedback. I had one hour for the meeting and we had to introduce each other for about ten minutes, and in the end, I had to give a feedback about her. Why don't they extend the appointment time for it?"

Hegel turned off his laptop and said to Li: "Rules are rules, we do not have a better choice to find a better solution, and we have to take it. You have to know, it is not our mother language. So we do not have an alternative way to figure the problem. What we can do and what we could do, in my humble opinion; is preparing for English better during the summer if you feel terrible in 112."

A few days later, Li went to the writing center for help, a day later he went to the writing center again. This time he had already finished his novel reflection. But Jonny did not follow the teacher's idea, his professor told him his writing contains more issues which should be fixed by revising himself. However Jonny did not think it is right, he thought it is unfair to international students, because there are three international students in his class, and two of them were told the same thing by the teacher. So Jonny did not know why he is not satisfied in 112 courses.

When Jonny went to class, his professor asked his English 109 teacher, he thought he should talk to him to know his English level. At night, Jonny received two emails from his previous 109 teachers and 112 teacher, they both suggested he take it later. Jonny did not know what to do, so he asked his academic adviser to see if she could give him advice. But in the morning, he checked his mailbox as routine; his adviser told him she had already emailed his 112 and 109 professors. She told him to take it later, and she recommended an English workshop for international students instead of English 112. At last he drooped the course after spring break. He did not figure out what is the standard requirement for taking the course; even he had a good grade on previous English lectures, and he was taking the writing studio to enhance his English writing skills.

There was only one month left for the final, everyone was preparing his or her last assignment. Hegel had a group assignment, to produce trailer for a movie which had already shown before. And Zack was playing his games with his friends; they had to work together to defeat the boss in the game and after he done that, his teacher required him to write a final reflection about the game, give advice to the designers for the puzzle, to make it more attractive for business purposes.

Li worked with his girlfriend, their assignment was creative work, he had to write a new chapter for one of the novel in the final chapter, which means they had to think about the plot, dialogue, scene and decide the happy ending or not. And Li decided to make a different translation before the final scene, he wanted the main character joined the darkness part first and then turn back in the end to become a hero, to save the people. He changed the scene from forest to North Pole, beyond that he altered the main purpose for the main character. The main character had a concussion in one battle in North Pole, he fell in the ocean, where people found him. He did not remember who he was, and his mission. After several months, he was taken by the main female character, which his girlfriend, who rescued him from the darkness side. Even his girlfriend helped him to remember who he was; he cannot remember anything from before. In the end, he led the battle to defeat the darkness, he concussed again and saved the world again. When he fell asleep, he found himself on his bed. Li's professor told him, the creative part requires more scene and dialogue to express the stressful atmosphere.

Zack and his classmates got through the game, his reflection analyzes if the game should be under control by the law, because some of the video games contains too much violence elements in the battle, and it is easy for children to forget real life and get addicted in the game world. Now it is the last day of finals week, they all finished the exam and assignment for their own. Only Jonny dropped the course, they decided to have fun uptown and before going back to China the next day. But there is something wrong with their planes and plan: they drank too much last night and they did not get the plane; secondly one of the students changed his grade on English department Nikka, so all their grades turned to be unknown until the school found a solution for this. So maybe they had to take 112 again in the next semester with the "Dropped Jonny".

Editorial Team's Note

In this piece, Jia Yao Wang uses an Inquiry Three assignment prompt inviting students to explore genre through remediation to communicate the unique challenges Miami's English 112 class presents for international student writers. Wang "remediates" the casual discourse of his peers in the genre of the short story. How does his writing – both in content and form – accomplish his larger goal of sharing the struggles and anxieties English language learners face in their first year of composition class? What audience does Wang attempt to reach and why does that matter? How might this creative work encourage change in our community? As you read the essay and reflection, consider Wang's use of alliteration, dialogue, and detail. What are the strengths of his writing and what changes might he make to better fit the genre of the short story?

Inquiry Four: Final Reflection

English 112 Portfolio

Andrew Frondorf

In reflecting on this past semester, I would like to say that this class has definitely helped me to reaffirm an interest within myself, that includes drawing connections between things. The conventional aesthetic of the comic forces the reader to connect two scenes, and I believe this sort of exercise has manifested itself in my desire to connect fields of geology, architecture, psychology, sociology, and other more niche interests, such as the uncanny valley.

For my first inquiry, I dove into what appeared to be the most abstract comic available, "H-Day" by Renee French, and I think this sort of comic allowed for the greatest degree of creative thought, as no words, and no meaning was spelled out in the form of text. Admittedly, I did actually read about the comic itself prior to analyzing it for inquiry one, and I do acknowledge that this sort of external awareness served to guide my thoughts, while they may have otherwise drifted against the winds of my own imagination. So in the future, I will consider that if I wish to get the most out of sinking my teeth into some form of surreal media.

This sort of experience took place for my other inquires as well, and I began to take a great deal of interest in how one's spatial circumstances serve to influence their internal thoughts/emotions. Additionally, I became, and continue to be, highly interested in the idea that a human being is a product of their environment. And so I began to discuss this with my best friend who is an architecture major, and he showed me a film. Everything about it is designed from the ground up to invoke psychological pain. The Berlin holocaust building.

If I were forced to point to a building that represents what I consider to be a sort of nihilism (but my understanding of nihilism is hilariously dismal), something that illustrates values that negate themselves, just examine the implications behind the design of this building. The entrance to the holocaust requires the visitor to enter in through a well illuminated, luxurious palace, giving of the aesthetic of royalty, permeating with the stench of faith. And the faith collapses under its own weight as the visitor is funneled downward into a cylindrical anus of an entrance, into darkness, and above this the visitor, the food making its path through the digestive tract of a monster, can just see a void, extending upward, like a sort of intestine, ultimately connected to an all-consuming darkness (and this brings to mind the hellish descent towards into the recesses of the gay BDSM club "rectum" in Irreversible, as the visitors hunt down the French rapist known as "the Tapeworm")

Another interesting component of the building is the six different large structural spaces within the interior, that no one can enter, and they can only be looked into through small windows. And German officials argued that the architect should remove the spaces from the building, because they must be heated, and yet no one can enter them, and so they pose an unnecessary cost, an unnecessary financial burden upon the city. And the architect replied in this sort of way: the holocaust is not something that can simply be forgotten with the existence of a museum, not something to just apologize for and move on from. The consequences of the event transcend time. There will always be a hellish residue, culminating from this event, one that every living thing will pay for, so long as life persists.

The architect explains his meaning behind the six large quarantined spaces running through the anatomy of the building. they're the permanent reminder of the Jewish heritage that was eradicated. But it is my belief that the inclusion of windows allows for a sort of misanthropic phenomenon to take place, wherein a person looking into the void, seeing nothing human until a face fills the window on the opposing wall, and this face is something that's always there to be looked into, through the windows, that face across from one another, into the eyes of another human being. The loss is always there. The violence always walking around, preserved in the bodymass around us, in the eyes of other human beings. The architect literally sticks it to humanity through forcing it to pay through the skin of its teeth to heat (constantly) uninhabited space, on German land. The whole experience of walking through that place, is meant to be a test. It's supposed to be a struggle. It's a sort of Kafkaesque hell.

This is why I love architecture so much. There's so much psychology to it. The space can be used as a weapon. The weapon inflicts a sort of intellectual wound, as the test amounts to one question: in my opinion, the "test" that Daniel Libeskind is referring to is not really a spatial test, it's pretty straightforward, it seems more like an emotional one. Even after walking through the exam, the traveler must decide whether or not they will choose to accept or reject mankind. And even if they should choose to accept those around them, there is ultimately no impersonal way of verifying that this is what counts a passing the test.

And so the test is absurd, in that there is no way of knowing the answer, no way of knowing one has passed, even after one has left the building.

In addition to analyzing architecture itself, the class spurred my interest in the act of abandoning a building, and what sorts of biological implication that might illustrate for a society. For example I considered writing an essay that would be a sort of philosophical/anthropological analysis of the connection between Thomas Ligotti and his birth/life in Detroit. I considered the idea of people being a product of their environmental circumstances.

Ligotti was born in the broken capital for unemployment, illiteracy, dropouts, and foreclosures. The sort of eerie place where you can literally buy a house that has nothing in it, for a few hundred dollars. A sort of urban organism teeming with resentment, deserted factories, deserted dreams, abandoned homes, forgotten people, and a sort of diseased environmental response, transmuting its nihilistic messages through some sort of metaphysical intestine, ultimately exiting through Ligotti's rectum of creativity, in the form of his textual filth.

In this way, the stories of Teatro Grottesco could be thought of as the digested residue of all the broken hopes that have been consumed by the passage of time, in Detroit.

References

http://www.youtube.com/watch?v=lQ6SPYaiST8
http://www.youtube.com/watch?v=_OYlkSukgKI
http://www.youtube.com/watch?v=u2fKtlQ05A0

Editorial Team's Note
Andrew Frondorf's essay reflects on his affinity for drawing connections between fields of study and personal interests. Frondorf draws from his interest in psychology in order to reflect upon the texts he

studied. He discusses how space and environment shape human beings. By using examples, he engages in a thoughtful critique of
architectural space, and explains how architectural spaces are designed for humans to move through them. The conclusion Frondorf
works toward is that it isn't just the spatial design that is key in architecture, but rather the emotional effects of spaces. At the end of his
essay, Frondorf considers other ideas he might explore in the future.
The major strengths of this reflective essay are the writer's willingness
to take creative risks, to experiment and map connections between
ideas, and to speculate on more avenues to explore in the future.

We have several great multi-modal reflections that could not be printed. Please visit the *CCM's* companion website to see all the different
ways reflection can be done (other than a print essay).

Dear Future Tina
Tina Kinstedt

Dear Future Tina,

English 112 has definitely taught me a great deal about analyzing English works. In addition, it has also taught me how to write proper analysis papers. In the beginning, I believed that telling the audience was enough, but now that I have reached the end of this semester, I have realized that showing is much more important. If you just tell an audience what you think without explaining your reasoning, they may be either confused or find other ways to interpret what you are saying. For this reason, I have finally learned how to correctly create an analytical piece. It only took me eighteen weeks. Better late than never I suppose.

After a semester in English 112, I have been able to better assess my strengths and weaknesses in English. I have realized that over the course of the semester I have become better at writing to a specific audience. In addition, I have learned that I am strong at conveying a specific message to my audience. I have also discovered that I am not great with organization. Often I start somewhere and end somewhere completely different or I end up writing in stream of consciousness type writing. I would definitely say structure is one of my weaknesses. However, after a semester in this class, I think I greatly improved on this aspect of my writing. I stopped using so much stream of consciousness writing and became more structured. It definitely took practice, but I really do believe it improved. I can now clearly see what I was thinking and where I wanted to go with my writing in my later inquiries.

I can't fully describe how much this class has taught me about myself. I learned about the best and worst aspects of my writing. In addition, I learned how to write a great paper and the meaning of audience. I've discovered that I need to start working sooner on some of my projects, because my third inquiry was just finished in time and I probably could have made it better if I had been smarter and worked ahead. I have also realized that I take way too much time to perfect something. On some of these inquiries I wrote drafts upon drafts for several days before I finally submitted my work. I think it made my work better, but it also subtracted from time I could have used to study other things. I can't always write the perfect paper. I realize that now.

In addition, I changed a lot during the different drafts of this inquiry. I first wrote an analytical paper to a peer audience, but then I realized that I wanted to make my work more personal and creative. For this reason, I changed my inquiry into a letter directed at myself. I added in humor and things that only I would quite understand in the hopes that whenever I read this in the future (theoretically right before sophomore year) I will actually enjoy what I am reading. In addition, I made sure that I wrote in different fonts and my favorite colors (blue and purple) for my portfolio so that I would find it more appealing. I get pretty bored after seeing the same color and font after so long. I wasn't quite sure how to tie it into the letter because I know that proper MLA format requires a specific font and black type. In addition, I was somewhat unsure if I wrote enough for the portfolio and exactly what to write in it. Hopefully I covered everything that was required.

I hope you like everything that I wrote to you, Future Me. I also hope you have become a millionaire. But I guess that's probably very improbable. But here's hoping.

Best Wishes,
Exam-Week-Freak-Out-Tina

Editorial Team's Note

For this particular Inquiry 4 portfolio reflection, student Tina Kinstedt was asked to address her past, present, or future self as writer while exploring her strengths and weaknesses in 112 and how she might utilize the insights gained in her first year of composition coursework. How does this particular audience affect her rhetorical choices? As you read the first reflection letter and final portfolio reflection, think about how and why Kinstedt creates a personal and humorous tone throughout. Though Kinstedt's piece in written as a letter to "Future Tina," where and how does it demonstrate use of many of the conventions of academic deductive writing.